ANIMAL
ULTIMATE HANDBOOK

NO LONGER PROPERTY OF
SEATTLE PUBLIC LIBRARY

D0469993

DK LONDON

Editor Kat Teece
US Editors Margaret Parrish, Jill Hamilton
US Senior Editor Shannon Beatty
Project Art Editor Charlotte Jennings
Design Assistant Holly Price
Editorial Assistant Kieran Jones
Managing Editor Jonathan Melmoth
Managing Art Editor Diane Peyton Jones
Senior Production Editor Nikoleta Parasaki
Production Controller Basia Ossowska
Publishing Coordinator Issy Walsh
Jacket Designers Charlotte Jennings
Publisher Francesca Young
Deputy Art Director Mabel Chan
Publishing Director Sarah Larter

DK DELHI

Senior Art Editor Nidhi Mehra
Project Art Editor Nehal Verma
Editor Niharika Prabhakar
Managing Editor Monica Saigal
Managing Art Editor Romi Chakraborty
Picture Researcher Geetika Bhandari
Senior DTP Designer Neeraj Bhatia
DTP Designer Sachin Gupta
Delhi Creative Heads Glenda Fernandes,
Malavika Talukder

First American Edition, 2022
Published in the United States by DK Publishing
1450 Broadway, Suite 801, New York, New York 10018

Copyright © 2022 Dorling Kindersley Limited
DK, a Division of Penguin Random House LLC
22 23 24 25 26 10 9 8 7 6 5 4 3 2 1
001–327031–July/2022
All rights reserved.

Without limiting the rights under the copyright reserved above,
no part of this publication may be reproduced, stored in or introduced
into a retrieval system, or transmitted, in any form, or by any means
(electronic, mechanical, photocopying, recording, or otherwise),
without the prior written permission of the copyright owner.
Published in Great Britain by Dorling Kindersley Limited.

A catalog record for this book is available from
the Library of Congress.
ISBN 978-0-7440-5669-3

DK books are available at special discounts when purchased in bulk for
sales promotions, premiums, fund-raising, or educational use.
For details, contact: DK Publishing Special
Markets, 1450 Broadway, Suite 801, New York, New York 10018
SpecialSales@dk.com

Printed and bound in China

For the curious
www.dk.com

MIX
Paper from
responsible sources
FSC™ C018179

This book was made with Forest
Stewardship Council™ certified paper –
one small step in DK's commitment to
a sustainable future. For more information
go to www.dk.com/our-green-pledge

ANIMAL
ULTIMATE HANDBOOK

Written by Andrea Mills, Lizzie Munsey,
Catherine Saunders,
Consultant Cathriona Hickey

Contents

MAMMALS

AMPHIBIANS

FISH

BIRDS

REPTILES

INVERTEBRATES

How this book works

Ready to read about the amazing members of the animal kingdom? Here is some information to help you find your way around this book.

Profiles

Animals from insects to mammals are introduced on these fact-packed profile pages. The profiles sit within different chapters, each focusing on an animal group.

Want to find out about a particular animal? Look it up in the index on pp. 346-351.

Super stats panels are filled with amazing information, including scientific name and location.

Not sure what a word means? Look it up in the glossary on pp. 342-345.

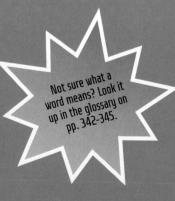

Extra images highlight a unique feature of the animal.

Head-to-head!

These pages feature competitions between two animals, whether it's a race or who can live the longest.

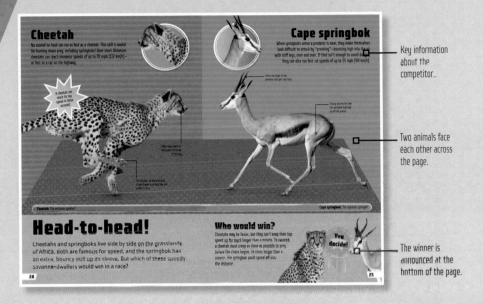

Key information about the competitor.

Two animals face each other across the page.

The winner is announced at the bottom of the page.

Special features

Feature pages give you extra information about the world of animals. How do creatures communicate? What is an invertebrate? Read on and find out.

Useful information about a subject, with pictures to help explain

What is an animal?

All the animals in existence have a few things in common. They eat, move, breathe, communicate, sense their surroundings, and reproduce. Plants and fungi can do some of these things, but not all of them.

Feeding

Energy is the force that animals use to do everything, from breathing to moving around. Animals get their energy from food—herbivores eat plants, carnivores eat meat, and omnivores eat both.

Sensing

Most animals have the five main senses that humans have: sight, hearing, taste, smell, and touch. Some animals have extra senses that we don't, which allow them to detect magnetism or electricity!

Snails are mollusks—a type of invertebrate.

Reptiles, such as crocodiles, are vertebrates.

Animal groups

Animals are divided into two main groups—vertebrates, which have backbones, and invertebrates, which don't. Vertebrates include mammals, birds, reptiles, amphibians, and fish.

There are more than 8 million types of animals in the world.

Communicating

Many animals are able to send messages to each other, for example, about food or danger. They might do this by making noises, or by leaving scent (smell) markings.

Moving

Most animals that live on land can move—they run, jump, and even fly. Many animals that live in water swim around, while others stay fixed to one spot, only moving their tentacles or other body parts.

Reproducing

All animals make copies of themselves by reproducing. Some lay eggs, while others give birth to living babies.

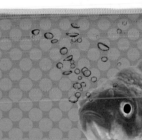

Breathing

All animals need oxygen to live. Some breathe it in from the air, while others take it in from water using special organs called gills.

Mammals

Our world is home to more than 6,400 different types of mammals! They come in all shapes and sizes, from tiny shrews to colossal elephants. Many of them live on land, but some live in the sea, such as dolphins and whales. All mammals have some things in common—they are warm–blooded, drink milk from their mothers, have similar internal skeletons, and have hairy bodies. Most mammal parents look after their babies when they are young.

What is a mammal?

Mammals are smart—they have big brains compared to their bodies and are able to form social relationships. But what else do they have in common?

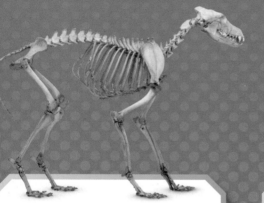

Bats are the only mammal that can really fly, although some other mammals are able to glide.

Inner skeleton

As vertebrates, mammals have bony skeletons inside their bodies. Although their sizes and shapes vary, mammal skeletons are all very similar, with a backbone, skull, and four limbs.

Warm blood

Mammals are warm-blooded—they generate heat themselves inside their bodies, which allows them to keep their body temperatures level.

Hairy skin

Some mammals don't have much hair, but they all have some, even elephants and whales! Many have a full coat of thick hair, called fur.

Milk

Mammal mothers feed their babies milk from glands in their skin. No other animal group produces milk in this way.

Living babies

Almost all mammals bear live young. That means they give birth to living babies, rather than laying eggs, like birds, for example.

The largest mammal is the blue whale—it is 110 ft (33 m) long and weighs up to 220 tons (200 metric tons)—that's more than 20 elephants!

Human mammals

Do these features seem familiar to you? That's because humans are mammals, too. The scientific name for our species is *Homo sapiens*, which means "wise man."

Sun bear

This bear climbs trees in search of its favorite food—insects. It rips open an ant nest or beehive, then slurps up the contents, including honey, insects, and their eggs.

Long tongue, for licking up ants

Light-colored fur around the nose and mouth

Weird, but true!
Sun bears are the smallest bears in the world, at around 80 lb (36 kg). That's the same weight as a labrador!

Short fur, so the bear doesn't overheat in its tropical home

Strong, curved claws

Super stats

Scientific name: Helarctos malayanus   **Life span:** Up to 25 years
Height: About 4¾ ft (1.4 m)   **Weight:** 60-150 lb (27-65 kg)
Diet: Fruit, birds, small rodents, insects
Habitat: Tropical rain forest   **Location:** Bangladesh, Brunei Darussalam, Cambodia, India, Indonesia, Lao People's Democratic Republic, Malaysia, Myanmar, Thailand, Vietnam

Giant panda

Only one food is any good to this bear—bamboo. Unfortunately, bamboo is not very nutritious. To get enough energy to survive, the panda must spend hours chewing. Any time it is not eating, it sleeps.

Powerful jaws and teeth for chomping away at bamboo

Black-and-white patterned fur

Big paws, specially designed for holding bamboo

Weird, but true!
A giant panda eats bamboo for up to 16 hours every day.

Super stats

Scientific name: Ailuropoda melanoleuca
Life span: Up to 20 years
Height: About 6 ft (1.8 m)   **Weight:** About 220 lb (100 kg)
Diet: Bamboo   **Habitat:** Temperate forests
Location: Southwest China

Guanaco

The guanaco lives at high altitudes in tough conditions. The air it breathes contains only small amounts of the oxygen its body needs. Luckily, its blood contains lots of red cells, which carry the oxygen around its body as quickly as possible.

Long ears

Weird, but true!
Tame, farmed guanacos are called llamas.

Thick, woolly coat for keeping warm

Two toes on each foot

Super stats

Scientific name: Lama guanicoe **Life span:** 20-25 years
Height: About 3½ ft (1.1 m) **Weight:** About 200 lb (90 kg)
Diet: Grasses, shrubs, herbs, lichens, fungi, cacti, and flowers
Habitat: Mountains, plateaus, plains, and coastlines
Location: The Andes mountains in South America

Dromedary camel

This camel is perfectly suited to life in the dry desert. It can keep water in its body by producing concentrated urine and dry dung, which helps it go for days without drinking water.

Super stats

Scientific name: Camelus dromedarius **Life span:** 40 years
Height: Up to 6½ ft (2 m)
Weight: 880–1,300 lb (400–600 kg)
Diet: Plants and saltbush
Habitat: Dry and desert areas
Location: Parts of Africa, Middle East, southwest Asia, and Australia

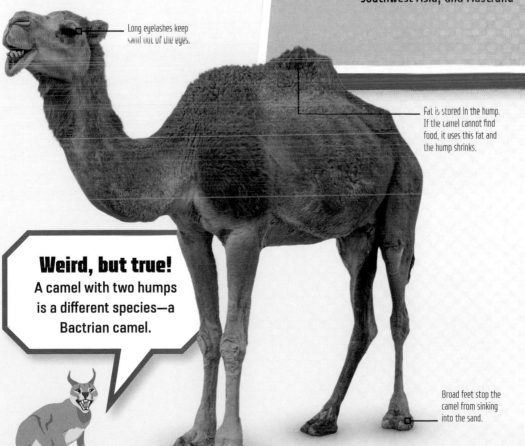

Long eyelashes keep sand out of the eyes.

Fat is stored in the hump. If the camel cannot find food, it uses this fat and the hump shrinks.

Weird, but true!
A camel with two humps is a different species—a Bactrian camel.

Broad feet stop the camel from sinking into the sand.

Vicuña

Graceful and light-bodied, the vicuña spends its time grazing in mountain grasslands. It lives in groups, which use poop to mark their territories.

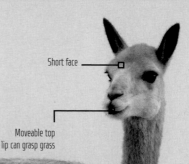

Short face

Moveable top lip can grasp grass

Thick coat of soft, fine wool

Weird, but true!
The vicuña's wool is so useful that it has been farmed for around 7,000 years.

Super stats

Scientific name: Vicugna vicugna   **Life span:** 15-20 years
Height: About 3 ft (90 cm)   **Weight:** About 110 lb (50 kg)
Diet: Low grasses
Habitat: Semiarid grasslands
Location: Andes mountains in Peru, Bolivia, Argentina, and Chile

African wild donkey

This donkey is tough! It eats spiked desert plants and can go without drinking water for up to three days at a time.

Long, pointed ears

Reddish-brown coat

Black stripes on legs, called leg bars

Slender legs, which are long compared to the body

Weird, but true!
The African wild donkey is the ancestor of the domestic donkey.

Super stats

Scientific name: Equus africanus   **Life span:** 20 years
Height: About 6½ ft (2 m)   **Tail length:** About 17 in (42 cm)
Weight: About 550 lb (250 kg)
Diet: Grasses
Habitat: Arid and semiarid bushland and grassland
Location: Eritrea, Ethiopia, and Somalia

African lion

A group of lions is called a pride. There is usually a head male and one or two other males. They defend the pride from other lions. Females work together to bring down prey for the pride to eat.

Weird, but true!
Lions are the only big cats that are able to kill animals bigger than they are.

The tuft at the end of the tail is used to communicate with other lions.

A thick, bushy mane helps the male attract females.

Claws can be pulled back into the paws when they are not in use.

Super stats

Scientific name: Panthera Leo   **Life span:** Up to 15 years
Length: Up to 7 ft (3 m)   **Tail length:** Up to 3 ft (1 m)
Weight: Up to 420 lb (190 kg)
Diet: Zebra, wildebeests, antelopes, and other herbivores
Habitat: Grasslands and deserts   **Location:** Sub-Saharan Africa

Leopard

High up in the branches of a tree, a leopard can survey the grassland, looking for prey. Once it has caught something, it drags the kill back up the tree, to keep it away from other predators.

Spots are clustered in rosette shapes.

Large head with powerful jaws

A long tail helps the leopard balance while climbing trees.

Weird, but true!
Leopards with black fur are called panthers.

Super stats

Scientific name: Panthera pardus **Life span:** Up to 12 years
Height: About 2¼–2½ ft (70–80 cm) **Tail length:** About 3 ft (90 cm)
Weight: Up to 200 lb (90 kg)
Diet: Warthogs, antelopes, baboons, and other animals **Habitat:** Forests, savannas, shrublands, grasslands, rocky areas, and deserts **Location:** Central, East and South Africa, and Eurasia

Cheetah

No animal on land can run as fast as a cheetah. This skill is useful for hunting down prey, including springboks! Over short distances cheetahs can reach immense speeds of up to 70 mph (112 km/h)— as fast as a car on the highway.

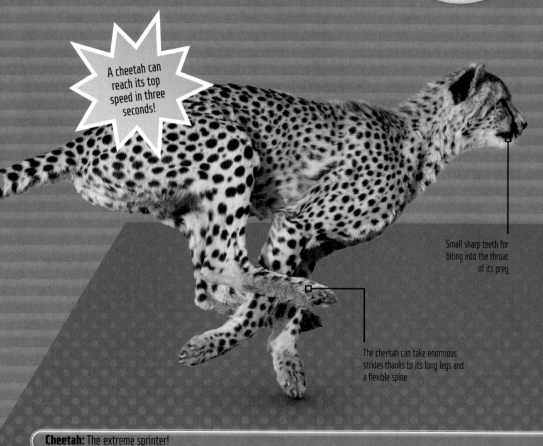

A cheetah can reach its top speed in three seconds!

Small sharp teeth for biting into the throat of its prey

The cheetah can take enormous strides thanks to its long legs and a flexible spine.

Cheetah: The extreme sprinter!

Head-to-head!

Cheetahs and springboks live side by side on the grasslands of Africa. Both are famous for speed, and the springbok has an extra, bouncy skill up its sleeve. But which of these speedy savanna–dwellers would win in a race?

Cape springbok

When springboks sense a predator is near, they make themselves look difficult to attack by "pronking"—bouncing high into the air with stiff legs, over and over. If that isn't enough to avoid danger, they can also run fast—at speeds of up to 55 mph (90 km/h).

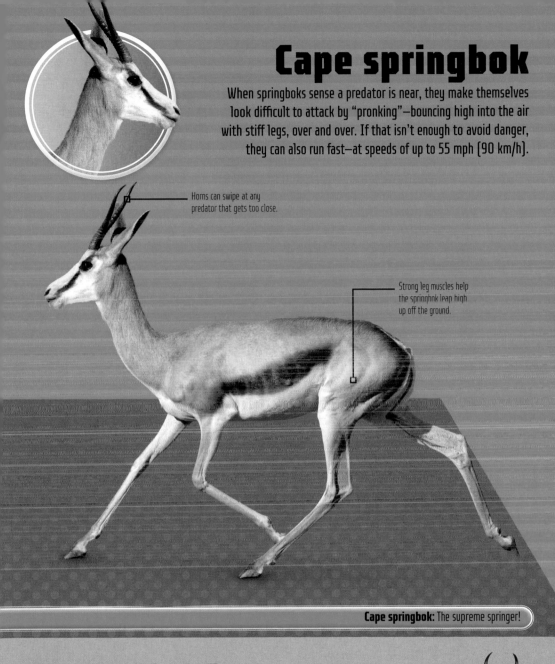

Horns can swipe at any predator that gets too close.

Strong leg muscles help the springbok leap high up off the ground.

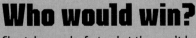

Cape springbok: The supreme springer!

Who would win?

Cheetahs may be faster, but they can't keep their top speed up for much longer than a minute. To succeed, a cheetah must creep as close as possible to prey before the chase begins. In races longer than a minute, the springbok could speed off into the distance.

You decide!

Ground pangolin

When a threat looms, this mammal rolls itself up into a tight ball, using its tough plates as armor to protect against the attacker.

Weird, but true!
The pangolin is the only mammal that has scales.

African wild dog

These dogs live in groups of up to 30 and hunt as a pack. The first dog to reach a prey animal bites into its nose, then keeps hold of it while the rest of the pack attacks.

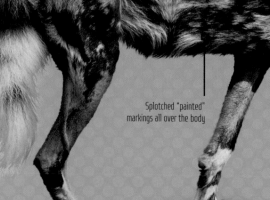

Splotched "painted" markings all over the body

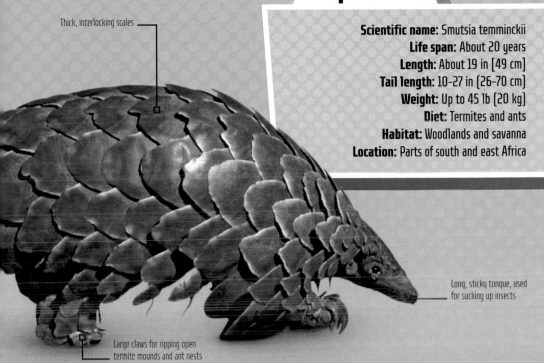

Thick, interlocking scales

Super stats

Scientific name: Smutsia temminckii
Life span: About 20 years
Length: About 19 in (49 cm)
Tail length: 10-27 in (26-70 cm)
Weight: Up to 45 lb (20 kg)
Diet: Termites and ants
Habitat: Woodlands and savanna
Location: Parts of south and east Africa

Long, sticky tongue, used for sucking up insects

Large claws for ripping open termite mounds and ant nests

Large, rounded ears

Super stats

Scientific name: Lycaon pictus
Life span: 10-12 years
Length: 2½-4½ ft (76-142 cm)
Tail length: Up to 3 ft (1 m)
Weight: 40-70 lb (18-31 kg)
Diet: Wildebeests, gazelles, and other animals
Habitat: Forest, grasslands, deserts
Location: Parts of south and east Africa

Sharp canine teeth, able to pierce thick skin

Weird, but true!
African wild dogs have four toes on each foot—one fewer than most dog species!

European hedgehog

A hedgehog curls up tightly if it is in danger. The curled hedgehog is a spiked ball—painful to touch and almost impossible for a predator to open.

Weird, but true!
An adult hedgehog has between 5,000 and 7,000 spines.

The face and belly are covered with hair, not spines.

Thick, spiked hairs called spines protect the hedgehog's body.

Wet black nose with a good sense of smell, for sniffing out insects

Super stats

Scientific name: Erinaceus europaeus   **Life span:** Up to 7 years
Length: 8½-10½ in (22-27 cm)   **Weight:** Up to 2½ lb (1.1 kg)
Diet: Small reptiles, birds' eggs, and carrion
Habitat: Temperate forests, woodlands, grasslands, and human settlements   **Location:** Mainland Europe, Britain and Ireland, and introduced to New Zealand

Meerkat

Standing bolt upright on its back legs, one meerkat in a group is always on guard. If it spots danger, it barks to warn the others to get to safety.

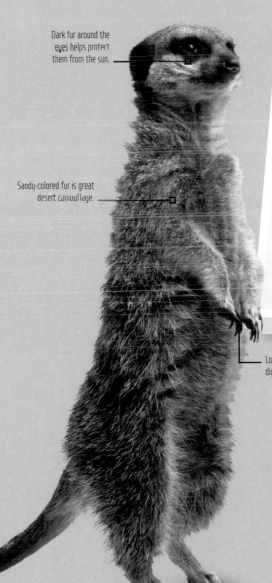

Dark fur around the eyes helps protect them from the sun.

Sandy-colored fur is great desert camouflage.

Long, strong claws for digging burrows

Super stats

Scientific name: Suricata suricatta **Life span:** 12-14 years
Length: 8½-10½ in (22-27 cm)
Tail length: About 7½ in (19 cm)
Weight: About 2 lb (1 kg)
Diet: Insects, lizards, birds, small snakes, and rodents
Habitat: Deserts and grasslands
Location: Southwest Africa

Weird, but true!
Meerkats like eating scorpions! They quickly bite off the tail first to keep from getting stung.

Wolverine

Super stats

Scientific name: Gulo gulo
Life span: 5-13 years
Length: 2-3 ft (65-90 cm)
Tail length: 5-10 in (13-26 cm)
Weight: 20-65 lb (9-30 kg)
Diet: Deer, sheep, small bears, and other animals **Habitat:** Boreal forests, tundra, and mountainous regions **Location:** Parts of Canada, the US, and northern Europe

Frozen landscapes are no problem for this tough mammal. Its jaws are so powerful that it can crunch through frozen carcasses.

Weird, but true!
Wolverines can smell so well that they know when an animal is hiding under the snow.

A double layer of fur repels water and keeps the animal warm in the snow.

Superstrong, bone-crushing jaws

Long claws help the wolverine walk on ice.

Brown-throated sloth

Slowly, slowly, slowly, and hanging upside down, the sloth inches along tree branches high up in the rain forest. In water, it is a surprisingly good swimmer, moving three times faster than it does on land.

Dark markings around the eyes

Curved claws for gripping onto branches

Thick, shaggy fur, often with green algae growing on it

Weird, but true!

Sloths only poop once a week. To do so, they make a slow journey all the way down to the forest floor.

Super stats

Scientific name: Bradypus variegatus
Life span: 30-40 years
Length: About 21 in (53 cm)   **Weight:** Up to 15 lb (7 kg)
Diet: Parts of Cercropia trees, including leaves, flowers, and fruits
Habitat: Tropical forests   **Location:** Central and South America

Cre sted porcupine

Sharp quills make the porcupine a formidable opponent. This large rodent can take on animals much bigger than itself, including lions! It charges backward, inflicting a face-full of spikes on any predator that doesn't get out of the way.

Quills are sharp, hardened hairs.

Weird, but true!
Porcupines can use their quills to spear predators if they are in danger.

Sharp teeth keep growing for the porcupine's whole life.

Strong claws, for digging

Super stats

Scientific name: Hystrix cristata
Life span: Up to 15 years
Length: 24-34 in (60-85 cm)   **Tail length:** 3½-6 in (8-15 cm)
Weight: Up to 65 lb (30 kg)   **Diet:** Roots, fruit, bark, and sometimes small animals   **Habitat:** Grassland, open woodland, and forest
Location: Parts of Africa and the Mediterranean

Duck-billed platypus

The platypus's strange rubbery bill has a special ability—it can sense the movements of tiny animals in the water. This allows the platypus to hunt even when it cannot see its prey, for instance, when worms are hidden in mud.

Ducklike bill

A sharp spike called a spur releases venom, used when attacking other males.

Webbed feet help the platypus speed through the water.

Weird, but true!
The platypus is one of only two mammals that lay eggs.

Super stats

Scientific name: Ornithorhynchus anatinus **Life span:** Up to 12 years
Length: 12-18 in (30-45 cm) **Tail length:** 4-6 in (10-15 cm)
Weight: 2-5 lb (1-2.3 kg)
Diet: Insect larvae, crayfish, shrimp, worms, snails, and other small fish
Habitat: Streams, rivers, and lakes
Location: Eastern Australia and Tasmania

Koala

The tree-loving koala has a superpower—it can eat eucalyptus leaves that are poisonous to other animals. In fact, eucalyptus leaves are the only thing it eats, chomping through up to 1 lb (450 g) of them every day.

Weird, but true!
Koalas can sleep for 21 hours a day.

Teeth designed for slicing and crushing leaves

Soft, long fur protects the koala from heat and rain.

Paws have sharp claws and rough pads for clinging to branches.

Super stats

Scientific name: Phascolarctos cinereus
Life span: About 15 years
Length: 24–33 in (60–85 cm)   **Weight:** Up to 31 lb (14 kg)
Diet: Leaves of the eucalyptus tree
Habitat: Eucalypt woodlands   **Location:** Eastern Australia

Red Kangaroo

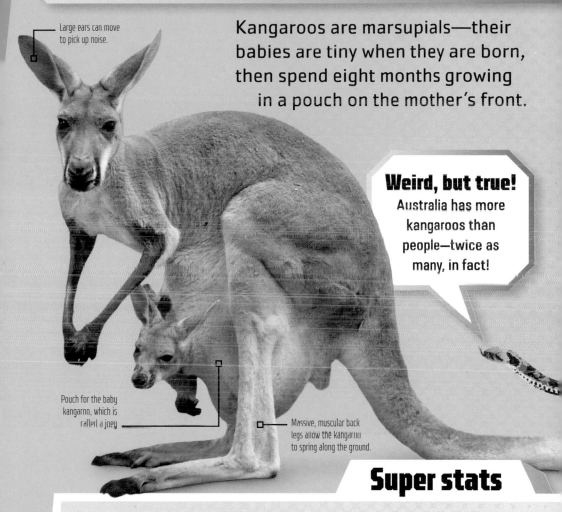

Large ears can move to pick up noise.

Kangaroos are marsupials—their babies are tiny when they are born, then spend eight months growing in a pouch on the mother's front.

Weird, but true!
Australia has more kangaroos than people—twice as many, in fact!

Pouch for the baby kangaroo, which is called a joey

Massive, muscular back legs allow the kangaroo to spring along the ground.

Super stats

Scientific name: Macropus rufus
Life span: Up to 20 years
Length: 3-5¼ ft (1-1.6 m)   **Tail length:** 35-44 in (90-110 cm)
Weight: Up to 200 lb (90 kg)   **Diet:** Grasses, shrubs, and foliage
Habitat: Scrubland and desert   **Location:** Australia

Bottlenose dolphin

These dolphins like each other's company. They live in groups, called pods, of up to 1,000 members! Dolphins ride along the ocean's surface, sometimes leaping up above the waves.

Weird, but true!
Every dolphin has its own unique whistle sound, which other dolphins are able to recognize.

Narwhal

Narwhal horns once seemed mysterious— they were thought to be unicorn horns! Actually, they aren't horns, but tusks— long, extended teeth.

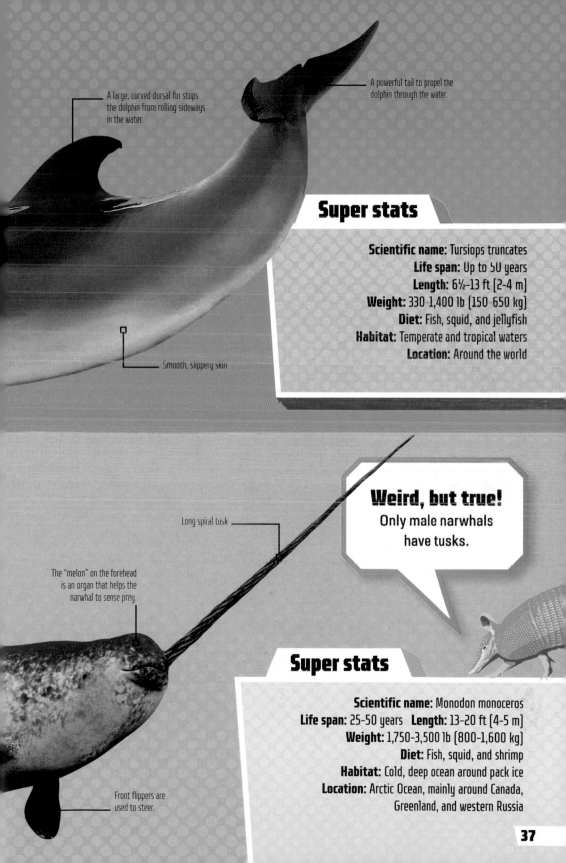

A large, curved dorsal fin stops the dolphin from rolling sideways in the water.

A powerful tail to propel the dolphin through the water.

Smooth, slippery skin

Super stats

Scientific name: Tursiops truncates
Life span: Up to 50 years
Length: 6½–13 ft (2–4 m)
Weight: 330–1,400 lb (150–650 kg)
Diet: Fish, squid, and jellyfish
Habitat: Temperate and tropical waters
Location: Around the world

Long spiral tusk

Weird, but true!
Only male narwhals have tusks.

The "melon" on the forehead is an organ that helps the narwhal to sense prey.

Super stats

Scientific name: Monodon monoceros
Life span: 25–50 years   **Length:** 13–20 ft (4–5 m)
Weight: 1,750–3,500 lb (800–1,600 kg)
Diet: Fish, squid, and shrimp
Habitat: Cold, deep ocean around pack ice
Location: Arctic Ocean, mainly around Canada, Greenland, and western Russia

Front flippers are used to steer.

Harbor seal

A seal spends most of its time in the water. It uses its back flippers to power itself along and its front flippers to steer.

Paddlelike flipper

A thick layer of fat called blubber helps the seal stay warm in cold water.

Walrus

Male walruses undertake fierce battles in order to win control of a group of females. They rear up at each other, using their sharp tusks to slice at their opponents.

A spiked mustache is used to feel for shellfish on the seabed.

Long curved tusks help the walrus haul itself out of the water.

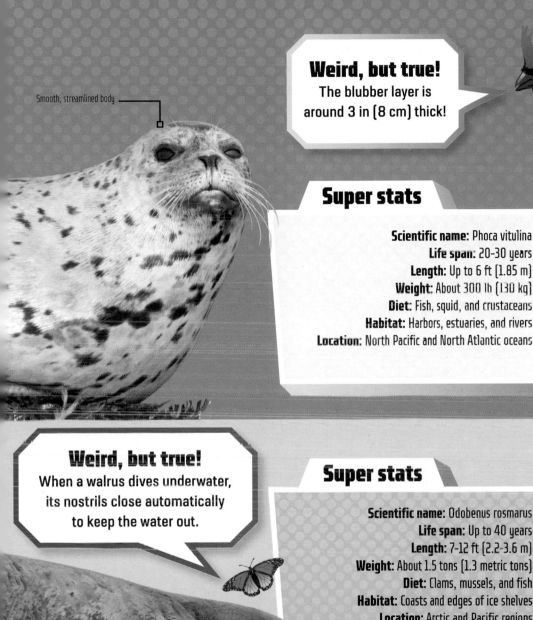

Smooth, streamlined body

Weird, but true!
The blubber layer is around 3 in (8 cm) thick!

Super stats

Scientific name: Phoca vitulina
Life span: 20–30 years
Length: Up to 6 ft (1.85 m)
Weight: About 300 lb (130 kg)
Diet: Fish, squid, and crustaceans
Habitat: Harbors, estuaries, and rivers
Location: North Pacific and North Atlantic oceans

Weird, but true!
When a walrus dives underwater, its nostrils close automatically to keep the water out.

Super stats

Scientific name: Odobenus rosmarus
Life span: Up to 40 years
Length: 7–12 ft (2.2–3.6 m)
Weight: About 1.5 tons (1.3 metric tons)
Diet: Clams, mussels, and fish
Habitat: Coasts and edges of ice shelves
Location: Arctic and Pacific regions

Wrinkled skin over a thick layer of blubber

Amazonian manatee

This manatee lives in the murky waters of the Amazon River and the rivers that flow into it. It is the only manatee that lives in freshwater—other species live in the ocean.

Large nose

Flippers for steering through the water.

Paddle-shaped tail

Super stats

Scientific name: Trichechus inunguis **Life span:** More than 12 years in captivity
Length: About 9⅛ ft (2.8 m)
Weight: About 992 lb (450 kg)
Diet: Water lettuce and hyacinth
Habitat: Freshwater rivers, swamps, and wetlands
Location: In the Amazon River, South America

Weird but true!
Manatees are not related to whales or seals, but to elephants!

Sea otter

The ocean is home for this otter. It spends its whole life at sea, hunting for crabs, fish, and spiky sea urchins.

Super stats

Scientific name: Enhydra lutris
Life span: Up to 20 years
Length: 4½–5 ft (1.4–1.5 m)
Tail Length: 9¾–13¾ in (25–35 cm)
Weight: 72–100 lb (33–45 kg)
Diet: Sea urchins, crabs, and mussels
Habitat: Coastal seas and kelp forests
Location: Northern coastal waters stretching from Kamchatka Peninsula, Russia to California and Alaska

Weird but true!
Sea otters sleep on their backs on the water's surface.

Long whiskers, for feeling for fish.

Two thick coats trap air, keeping the otter warm.

Webbed feet help them swim quickly.

Snow Leopard

The pale coat and dark markings on this big cat help it to hide among the snow and rock of its mountain habitat—so it can creep up on prey!

Weird but true!
Snow leopards cannot roar. Instead they hiss or growl.

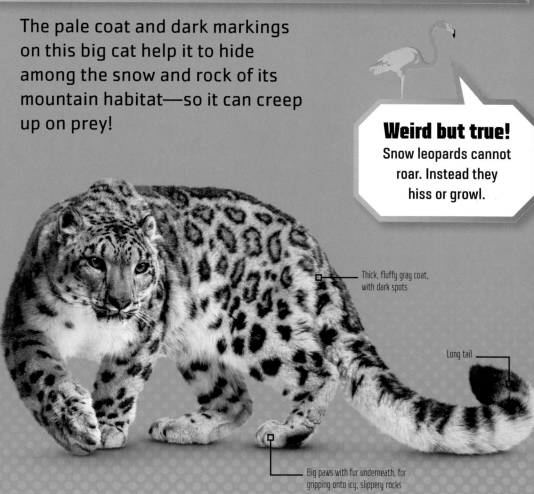

Thick, fluffy gray coat, with dark spots

Long tail

Big paws with fur underneath, for gripping onto icy, slippery rocks

Super stats

Scientific name: Panthera uncia
Lifespan: About 11 years
Length: 29½–59 in (75–150 cm) **Weight:** 132–397 lb (60–180 kg)
Diet: Blue sheep, Argali wild sheep, ibex, marmots, pikas, deer, and other small mammals **Habitat:** High mountains **Location:** Southern Russia, Mongolia, China, Afghanistan, Pakistan, India, and Nepal

Caracal

You can recognize this small cat by its distinctive ear tufts. The caracal is an excellent jumper—it can leap to catch birds that have just taken flight from the ground!

Super stats

Scientific name: Caracal caracal
Lifespan: About 12 years
Length: 33-48 in (83 123 cm)
Weight: 25-40 lb (9.5-18 kg)
Diet: Birds, rodents, and small antelopes
Habitat: Woodlands, savannas, and scrub forests
Location: Africa and Middle East

Tufted ears, sensitive to sound

Sandy colored coat

Fairly short tail, compared to other wild cats

Weird but true!

Caracals have such good hearing that they can hear a mouse's footsteps.

Puma

Powerful and strong, pumas are good at climbing, swimming, jumping, and running fast. They cover huge distances when they are hunting their prey.

Thick fur coat

Strong, muscular body

Short, powerful legs

Amur tiger

This fearsome feline is the largest cat of all. It lives in the icy tundra of eastern Russia and northern China.

Weird but true!
The Amur tiger weighs up to 675 lb (300 kg)—that's as much as four adult men.

Long thick tail with even stripes

Super stats

Scientific name: Puma concolor
Life span: Up to 13 years **Length:** About 4 ft (1.2 m)
Tail Length: 24¾-37¾ in (63-96 cm)
Weight: 92½-136 lbs (42-62 kg)
Diet: Mammals, such as deer and rabbits
Habitat: Desert scrub, chaparral, swamps, and forests
Location: Southeastern Alaska to
southern Argentina and Chile

Weird but true!

Pumas can leap a long
way, covering 40 ft
(12 m) in a single jump.

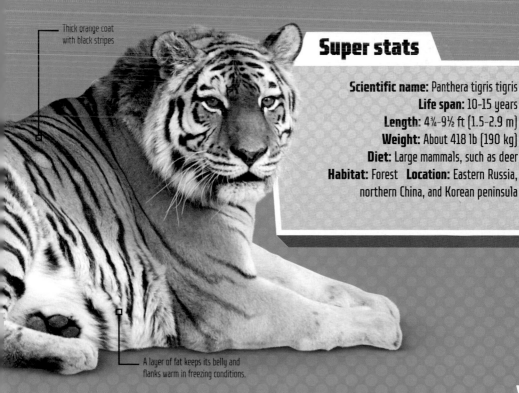

Thick orange coat
with black stripes

Super stats

Scientific name: Panthera tigris tigris
Life span: 10-15 years
Length: 4¾-9½ ft (1.5-2.9 m)
Weight: About 418 lb (190 kg)
Diet: Large mammals, such as deer
Habitat: Forest **Location:** Eastern Russia,
northern China, and Korean peninsula

A layer of fat keeps its belly and
flanks warm in freezing conditions.

The watering hole

Why might elephants, zebras, and springboks gather at spots like this one in Namibia? In the dry season, many of the rivers and ponds in savannas dry up. All animals need to drink, so they flock to the few places where water remains.

Merriam's kangaroo rat

Born to bounce, this desert-dwelling rat hops around from place to place. It can leap an incredible 9 ft (2.75 m) in a single jump. If danger threatens, it bounds out of the way.

If humans could jump 130 times our height, we'd be able to spring onto the roof of a 60-story building.

Long tail helps balance out bounces

Large back legs and feet allow kangaroo-like hopping

Merriam's kangaroo rat: The leaping rat!

Head-to-head!

Two famously spring–legged challengers are ready to compete! They're both known for their incredible leaps, but which is the highest jumper of all?

Cat flea

This insect lives cosily in the fur of pet cats, drinking their blood. It uses giant leaps to spring between animals, covering up to 13½ in (34 cm) at a time.

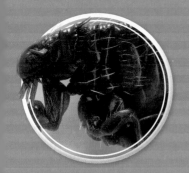

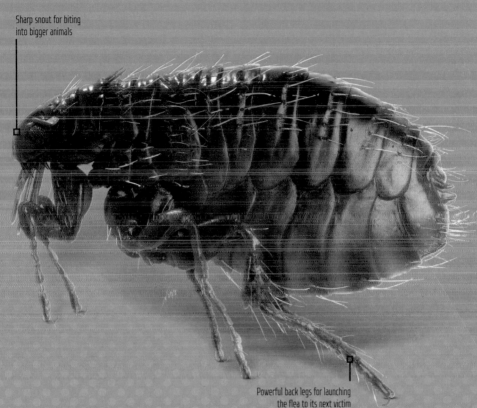

Sharp snout for biting into bigger animals

Powerful back legs for launching the flea to its next victim

Cat flea: A vampire on springs!

Who would win?

The rat can jump further than the flea. But if you account for their body size the flea would win—it jumps 130 times its body length, while the rat only leaps 55 times its length.

You decide!

Proboscis monkey

This long-nosed monkey lives in rainforests, and never strays far from the water. It is an excellent swimmer, and can swim up to 65 ft (20 m) underwater if needed.

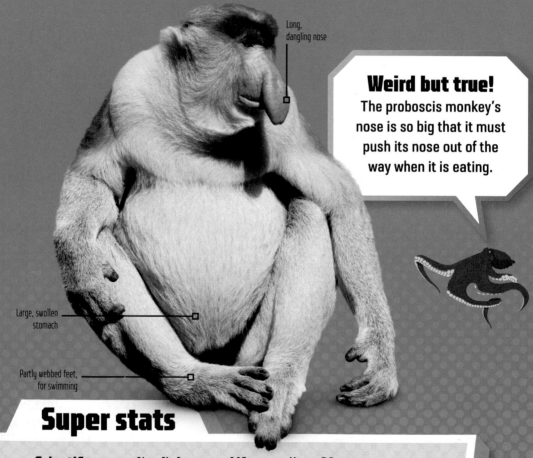

Long, dangling nose

Weird but true!
The proboscis monkey's nose is so big that it must push its nose out of the way when it is eating.

Large, swollen stomach

Partly webbed feet, for swimming

Super stats

Scientific name: Nasalis larvatus   **Lifespan:** Up to 20 years
Length: 22-28 in (56-72 cm)   **Tail length:** 22-29 in (56-75 cm)
Weight: 22-44 lb (10-20 kg)
Diet: Leaves, seeds, unripe fruits, and occasionally insects
Habitat: Swampy mangrove forests and rivers
Location: Forests on the Indonesian Island of Borneo

Emperor tamarin

High in the treetops, this mustachioed tamarin bounds between branches, in search of insects and fruit. It often lives in mixed groups with other types of tamarins.

Long, drooping white moustache

Weird but true!
Tamarins almost always have twin babies. They are carried around by the father, apart from when they are being fed by their mother.

Tail is twice as long as the rest of the body

Narrow, clawed hands for snatching insects from twigs and leaves

Super stats

Scientific name: Saguinus imperator **Life span:** 10-20 years
Length: 9-10 in (23-26 cm)
Tail length: 13¾-16½ in (35-42 cm)   **Weight:** About 1⅛ lb (0.5 kg)
Diet: Mainly fruit, but also insects, gum, nectar, and leaves
Habitat: Lowland and mountain rain forests, seasonally flooded forests
Location: Southeast Peru, northwest Bolivia, and northwest Brazil

These primates can only be found in one place on Earth—on the island of Madagascar. Most lemurs prefer to spend their time in the treetops, but this striped–tailed species is often found on the forest floor.

Strong hind legs allow the ring-tailed lemur to jump from the ground into trees.

The ring-tailed lemur holds its eye-catching, striped tail straight up in the air to tell others to follow along.

Super stats

Scientific name: Lemur catta
Life span: About 16 years
Height: About 1½ ft (46 cm)
Tail Length: Up to 2 ft (61 cm)
Weight: 5½–7½ lb (2½–3½ kg)
Diet: Leaves, fruit, and flowers
Habitat: Open areas and forests
Location: Southwestern Madagascar

Weird but true!

Males make foul-smelling substances in special glands. They rub their tails in the smell to wave at rivals in "stink fights."

A reflective layer in the eye allows for better vision at night.

On the ground, ring-tailed lemurs move on all fours most of the time.

Slow loris

It looks cute, but this little primate is poisonous! It is the only poisonous mammal, producing venom from a special gland near its elbow.

Super stats

Scientific name: Nycticebus
Life span: About 17 years
Lengtht: 10-15 in (26-38 cm)
Tail Length: 2 in (5 cm)
Weight: 2½ lb (1.2 kg)
Diet: Birds, lizards, and fruit
Habitat: Tropical forests
Location: Southeast Asia

Weird but true!
Mother lorises lick their babies, covering them in a protective layer of poisonous spit

Thick, soft brown fur

Enormous eyes, for seeing in the dark.

Long-fingered hands help it grip tree branches.

Quokka

The quokka is a mini kangaroo. It bounces around on its back legs and comes out to feed at night.

Mouth appears to be smiling.

Pouch for a baby quokka, called a joey.

Strong back legs

Weird but true!
Most quokkas live in one place—Rottnest Island in Australia.

Super stats

Scientific name: Setonix brachyurus
Life span: About 10 years
Height: 16-21½ in (40-54 cm)   **Tail Length:** 10-14 in (25-35 cm)
Weight: 5½-1 lb (2.5-5 kg)   **Diet:** Leaves, grasses, and fruit
Habitat: Thick forest, open woodland, low scrub, and swamp edges or river banks   **Location:** Southwest Australia

Southern giraffe

Giraffes are perfectly adapted to feed from the very tops of trees. Their long necks let them reach up, and their long flexible tongues can pluck leaves from between the thorns of acacia trees.

Super stats

Scientific name: Giraffa giraffa
Life span: 20-25 years
Height: Around 13-16.5 ft (4-5 m)
Tail Length: Up to 8 ft (2.4 m)
Weight: Up to 3,000 lb (1,360 kg)
Diet: Leaves, seeds, fruits, buds, and branches high up in mimosa and acacia trees
Habitat: Open woodland and wooded grassland
Location: West to east Africa

Big eyes help the giraffe see a long way.

Long neck for feeding from the tops of trees.

Towering, slender legs

Weird but true!

Giraffes have the same number of bones in their necks as us—seven. But theirs are much longer!

American bison

This massively built animal has a large head, thick neck, and a generally heavy in the front look. Males use their powerful bodies to fight each other in the breeding season.

Super stats

Scientific name: Bison bison
Life span: 10-20 years
Length: 7-11 ft (2.1-3.5 m)
Tail Length: 1-2 ft (30-80 cm)
Weight: 770-2,200 lb (350-1,000 kg)
Diet: Plants, such as grasses, lizards, and fruit **Habitat:** Mountains, forests and grasslands **Location:** West and north North America

Weird but true!

Huge herds of bison used to roam the American grasslands, but many of them were killed by hunters in the 19th century.

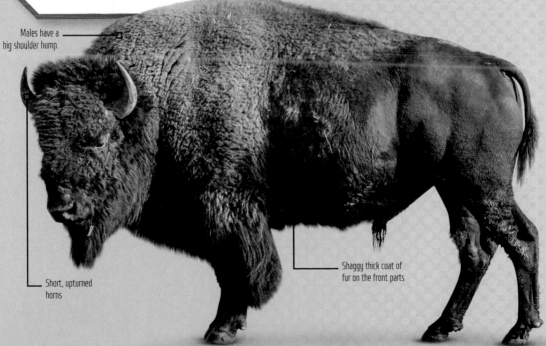

Males have a big shoulder hump.

Short, upturned horns

Shaggy thick coat of fur on the front parts

Grizzly bear

Big-bodied and powerful, this massive bear is a fierce carnivore. But it doesn't just eat meat—it is known for scooping salmon out of streams and will also nibble on berries, plants, and nuts.

Weird but true!
Grizzlies hibernate for around half the year, without eating or drinking.

Super stats

Scientific name: Ursus arctos horribilis
Life span: About 25 years
Height: Up to 9 ft (2.8 m)
Weight: Up to 900 lb (410 kg)
Diet: Fruits, plant, meat, and fish
Habitat: Forests, alpine meadows, and prairies with access to coastal areas, rivers, or streams
Location: North America

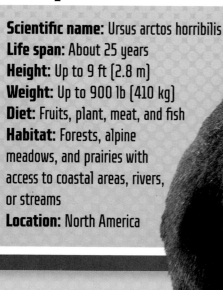

Nonspecialized teeth for eating whatever the bear can catch

Thick brown hair with silver tips

Long, strong claws for catching fish and digging

Polar bear

Ice and snow are no problem for this Arctic-living bear. It spends its time hunting seals and swimming through the icy water between chunks of sea ice.

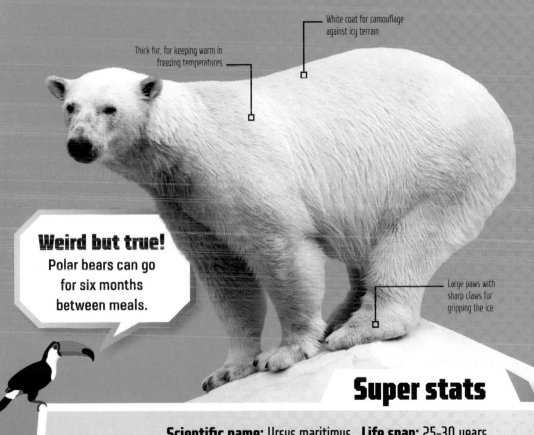

White coat for camouflage against icy terrain

Thick fur, for keeping warm in freezing temperatures

Large paws with sharp claws for gripping the ice

Weird but true!
Polar bears can go for six months between meals.

Super stats

Scientific name: Ursus maritimus   **Life span:** 25-30 years
Height: 6½-8¼ ft (2-2.5 m)   **Weight:** Up to 1,600 lb (725 kg)
Diet: Seals, seabirds, caribou, fish, and sometimes vegetation
Habitat: Arctic pack ice and tundra
Location: Coastlands and islands of the Arctic region

Moose

The mighty moose is the biggest deer in the world. After spending the summer alone when food is plentiful, it travels with other moose in winter to look for new food supplies.

Weird but true!

Male moose regrow their antlers every year. They fall off in winter and grow back in the summer.

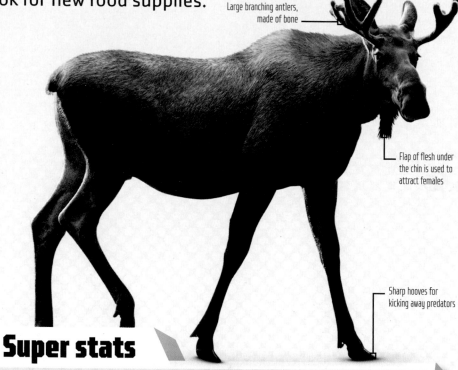

Large branching antlers, made of bone

Flap of flesh under the chin is used to attract females

Sharp hooves for kicking away predators

Super stats

Scientific name: Alces alces   **Life span:** 15–20 years
Length: 8–10½ ft (2.5–3.2 m)   **Weight:** 1,800 lb (816 kg)
Diet: Leaves, stems, twigs, and the bark of small shrubs
Habitat: Marshy forests **Location:** Northern parts of North America, Europe, and Asia

Reindeer

Paddle-shaped front part of antlers is used for scraping away ice and snow.

Also called the caribou, this deer is at home in the snow. It spends its life on the move, in a huge herd, looking for food. Some reindeer herds travel up to 750 miles (1,200 km) every season.

Long antlers vary in size between individuals.

Two layers of fur, to trap heat

Weird but true!
Female reindeer are the only female deer that have antlers.

Wide hooves, to stop the deer from sinking into the snow

Super stats

Scientific name: Rangifer tarandus   **Life span:** 15–20 years
Length: 4–7¼ ft (1.2–2.2 m)   **Weight:** Up to 700 lb (317 kg)
Diet: Mosses, herbs, lichens, fungi, ferns, grasses, shoots, and leaves
Habitat: Mountain tundra and coniferous forests
Location: The Arctic tundra and neighboring forests of Greenland, Scandinavia, Russia, Alaska, and Canada

Etruscan shrew

This tiny rodent is one of the world's smallest mammals and is lighter than a bumblebee! It is active throughout the day and night, resting for a few hours at a time.

Thin tail, without any fur

Weird but true!
A female Etruscan shrew can have up to six litters of babies every year.

Kitti's hog-nosed bat

Caves are home for this bat, which is the smallest in the world. It sleeps in groups of around 100, coming out of its cave at dawn and dusk to hunt for tiny insects.

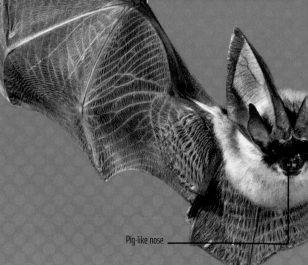

Pig-like nose

Long, pointed nose

Brown, furry body

Super stats

Scientific name: Suncus etruscus
Life span: About 2 years **Length:** 2½–4 in (6–10 cm)
Weight: About 0.1 oz (2 g)
Diet: Insects, worms, snails, and spiders
Habitat: Shrubs **Location:** Southern Europe,
South to Southeast Asia, Sri Lanka, North to East
Africa, and West Africa

Super stats

Scientific name: Craseonycteris thonglongyai
Life span: 5–10 years
Length: 1–1¼ in (3–3.5 cm)
Weight: ⅛ oz (2 g)
Diet: Insects **Habitat:** Caves
Location: Thailand and Myanmar

Large, sensitive ears to
help listen out for prey

Wings made of thin,
leathery skin stretched
across long, bony fingers

Weird but true!

This bat is sometimes called a bumblebee
bat due to its tiny size—it is small enough
to perch on a human fingertip!

Communication

Animals stay in touch with each other in the same way we do. Communicating lets them find mates, work together, avoid fights, and share information about food or danger.

Touch

Many animals touch each other to build bonds, or for reassurance. Bonobos groom each other to strengthen their relationships, which is important when you live in a group.

Grooming means removing insects and other unwanted things from each other's fur.

Wolves howl to communicate with their pack.

Sound

Animal sounds aren't just noise—each sound means something to the animal that makes it, and can be understood by other animals of the same species. They may make a sound that means "danger is near," for example.

Chemical

Some reptiles use chemicals to communicate. Male lizards have glands on the insides of their legs that produce special chemicals. These are like messages about themselves that other lizards can understand.

Lizards pick up each others' chemicals using their tongues.

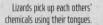

Branches and other items are used to build.

Visual

Some animals communicate using visual clues, such as their body markings, or even by glowing in the dark. The male bower bird builds elaborate displays of colorful objects to try to attract a mate.

Przewalski's horse

This is the world's last wild horse. It lives in herds, roaming grassy plains in search of grasses to graze on.

Super stats

Scientific name:
Equus ferus przewalskii
Life span: Up to 36 years
Length: 7¼–9 ft (2.2–2.8 m)
Weight: Up to 900 lb (408 kg)
Diet: Grass, leaves, buds
Habitat: Grassy plains
Location: Mongolia

Weird but true!
These horses have sharp frontal teeth shaped like chisels, for slicing up grass.

Heavy head with small ears

Bristly upright mane

Tail is used to flick away flies.

Short strong legs with tough hooves

Plains zebra

Zebras gather in large herds, which roam across the central African grasslands. Living in big groups makes it harder for predators, such as lions, to attack them.

Super stats

Scientific name: Equus quagga
Life span: About 25 years
Height: 4¼ ft (1.3 m)
Tail Length: 1½–1¾ ft (47–56.5 cm)
Weight: 850 lb (385 kg)
Diet: Grasses
Habitat: Open grasslands and savannas **Location:** Eastern and southern parts of Africa

Long, stripy, crest-like mane

Weird but true!

Each zebra has a pattern of stripes that is unique to them, in the same way human fingerprints are.

Black-and-white stripes on body

Strong hooves are used to kick at predators.

Blue whale

This gigantic creature is the largest animal to have ever lived on Earth—much bigger than any dinosaur. Its heart is the size of a small car, and its tongue is so massive an adult male elephant could sit on it.

Blowhole for breathing in and out

Enormous mouth with comblike plates, called baleen plates, to trap krill

Each eye is the size of a grapefruit.

Each whale has individual skin markings that are as unique as human fingerprints.

Scientific name: Balaenoptera musculus
Life span: 80-90 years
Length: Up to 105 ft (32 m)
Weight: Up to 200 tons (180 tonnes)
Diet: Mainly krill   **Habitat:** Oceans
Location: All oceans apart from Arctic

The tail is split into two sections, called flukes.

Weird but true!

A blue whale needs to eat about 4 million tiny shrimp, called krill, every day!

Giant flippers for changing direction

Dom sticated anim ls

People have lived closely with animals for thousands of years. Over time, this relationship and breeding by humans means the animal changes and is a new species altogether.

Cats

Cats have been kept as pets for more than 7,000 years. They are useful hunters to have around, eating pests such as mice and rats.

Dogs

The first tame dogs helped early people hunt animals around 15,000 years ago, or even earlier! Today, they are mainly popular as pets.

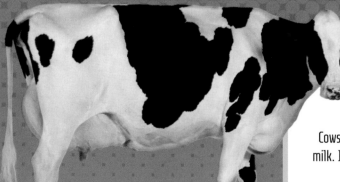

Cattle

Cows are farmed for their meat and milk. In the past, they were also used to pull heavy carts.

Horses

Before motor vehicles, horses were an important form of transportation. We now have quicker ways to get around, but some people still ride horses for fun.

Chickens

The original chicken was the red jungle-fowl, which lives in jungles in Asia. Now there are hundreds of different types of tame chickens. They are kept for their meat and eggs.

Wild horses had fewer coat colors than modern, domesticated horses.

Llamas

Descended from the wild guanaco, llamas are originally from South America. They can carry heavy loads and are farmed for their wool, milk, and meat.

Bees

For a long time people helped themselves to the honey of wild bees. Now, bees are farmed—people build and take care of bee hives, then harvest the honey and wax.

Eastern lowland gorilla

Mighty gorillas live in family groups led by the biggest male, who is called the silverback. The silverback protects his family from predators and fights off any rival males.

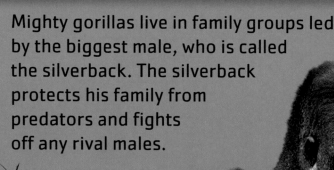

Heavyset body, with wide chest and shoulders

Weird but true!
Gorillas make nests to sleep in at night, and the females snuggle up with their young.

Hands are like a human's, but stronger and hairier.

Super stats

Scientific name: Gorilla beringei graueri
Life span: 35-50 years
Height: 4-5½ ft (1.2-1.67 m)   **Weight:** Up to 440 lb (200 kg)
Diet: Stems, bamboo shoots, and fruits
Habitat: Tropical rainforests
Location: Eastern Democratic Republic of Congo (DRC)

Sum tran orangut n

Rain forests are home for this great ape. It lives high up in the canopy, swinging between trees in search of insects, eggs, and fruit.

Super stats

Scientific name: Pongo abelii
Life span: Up to 45 years
Height: 4-5 ft (1.2-1.5 m)
Weight: 66-198 lb (30-90 kg)
Diet: Plant matter, such as fruit and bark, and insects
Habitat: Tropical forests
Location: Northern part of the Indonesian island of Sumatra

Weird but true!

Orangutans use twigs to get food, scooping insects out of their nests and honey out of beehives.

Long, orange-colored fur

Long arms help the orangutan swing through the trees.

The feet are similar to the hands, with long toes that can grip branches.

Common chimpanzee

These clever apes live in family groups of up to 30. They work together to hunt, and even wage war on other groups of chimpanzees.

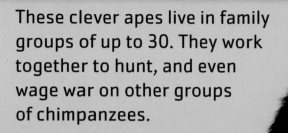

Bare skin on face

Black fur covers most of the body.

Weird but true!
Chimpanzees are the animals most closely related to humans.

Hands have gripping thumbs, which allow a precise grip.

Super stats

Scientific name: Pan troglodytes
Life span: 45 years
Weight: 44-200 lb (20-70 kg)   **Height:** Up to 5.5 ft (1.7 m)
Diet: Fruit, leaves, flowers, and seeds
Habitat: Tropical forests and savannas
Location: Central Africa

Human

Humans first appeared in Africa around 250,000 years ago. They spread around the world from there, and now live on every continent, often in big cities.

Nostrils are close together compared to other apes.

Weird but true!
The world is home to nearly 8 billion humans.

Hands have inward-facing thumbs, for gripping.

Super stats

Scientific name: Homo sapiens
Life span: Average life expectancy is 66 years
Weight: Average 176 lb (80 kg)
Height: Average 5 ft 7 in (170 cm)
Diet: Omnivores
Habitat: All environments
Location: Worldwide

The feet are flatter than the hands, and allow humans to stand upright.

American pygmy shrew

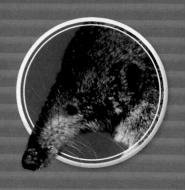

Weighing only ³⁄₁₆ oz (2 g), this is the smallest mammal in North America. It is constantly on the hunt for food, such as insects, spiders, and other miniscule animals. It catches and eats a prey animal every 15 to 30 minutes.

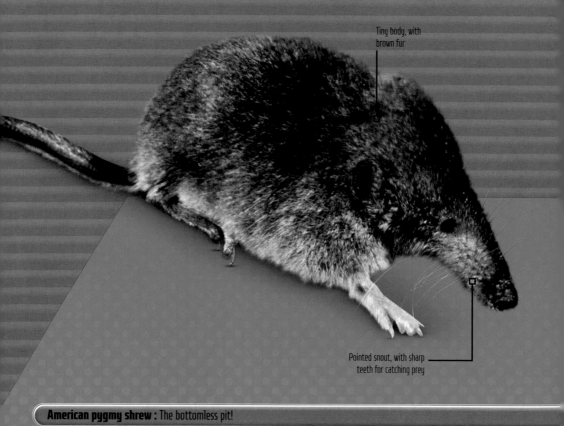

Tiny body, with brown fur

Pointed snout, with sharp teeth for catching prey

American pygmy shrew : The bottomless pit!

Head-to-head!

These two contenders are tiny in size but huge in appetite. To keep their tiny bodies going, they must constantly search for food. So, which of them is the biggest eater of all?

Bee hummingbird

This tiny bird is the world's smallest, weighing in at a mere $\frac{3}{16}$ oz (2 g). It flits around drinking sugary nectar from flowers. Bee hummingbirds visit thousands of flowers every day, and feed every 10 or 15 minutes.

Short, pointed bill, for poking into flowers

Tiny body, with a short tail

Bee hummingbird nests are tiny, at 1 in (2.5 cm) wide—and their eggs are the size of peas.

Bee hummingbird: The nectar drinker!

Who would win?

The two animals weigh the same, but the shrew is the bigger eater—it eats three times its body weight every day, while the hummingbird only eats half. Both species can starve to death in only hours if they can't find food.

Winner!

Capybara

The capybara is about the same size as a pig, which makes it the world's largest rodent. It grazes on grass on the land, but spends a lot of its time in rivers. If danger threatens, it leaps into the water and swims to safety.

Weird but true!
Capybaras' teeth keep growing all their lives.

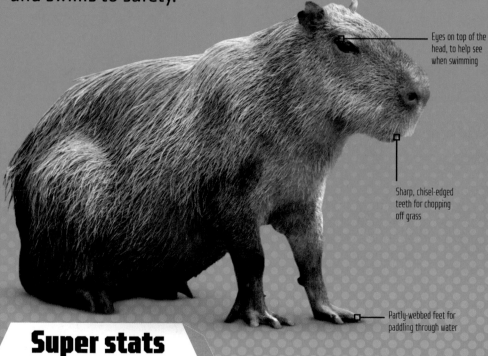

Eyes on top of the head, to help see when swimming

Sharp, chisel-edged teeth for chopping off grass

Partly-webbed feet for paddling through water

Super stats

Scientific name: Hydrochoerus hydrochaeris   **Life span:** About 10 years
Length: About 4¼ ft (1.3 m)   **Weight:** 77-143 lb (35-65 kg)
Diet: Mainly grasses and aquatic plants, but also grain and melons
Habitat: Flooded grasslands and riverside forests
Location: South America, east of the Andes mountains

Short-tailed chinchilla

Despite being small and cute, this rodent is also tough—it lives in freezing cold conditions, high up in the mountains. Its soft fur, adorable appearance, and friendly nature make the chinchilla a popular pet.

Super stats

Scientific name: Chinchilla brevicaudata
Life span: 8-10 years
Length: 11-19 in (28-49 cm)
Weight: Up to 2 lb (1 kg)
Diet: Vegetation
Habitat: Burrows in mountain scrubland **Location:** Throughout the Andes mountains of northwest Argentina, Chile, Peru, and Bolivia

Weird but true!

Chinchillas have very thick fur—each of their hair follicles holds about 60 hairs.

Whiskers act as feelers in the dark

Gray coloring to help blend in with rocks

Thick, bushy tail

Mountain goat

The mountain goat is an expert climber. It can climb the steepest slopes, walking with ease along tiny cracks in the rock. Where there are gaps between rocks, the goat leaps effortlessly across them.

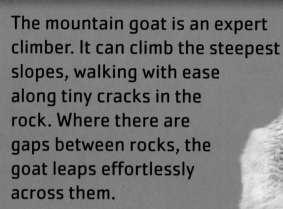

Small, curved horns

Thick fur to protect against freezing weather conditions

Rubberlike sole for gripping uneven ground

Weird but true!
Baby mountain goats can climb, leap, and run just minutes after they are born.

Super stats

Scientific name: Oreamnos americanus **Life span:** 9-12 years
Height: About 3¼ ft (1 m) **Weight:** About 260 lb (120 kg)
Diet: Alpine firs and conifers, grasses, herbs, foliage, twigs, and lichens
Habitat: Mountain ranges
Location: North America

Malayan tapir

The tapir spends its days hidden away in thick bushes. At night, it comes out to look for food, using its flexible snout to pick leaves and fruit.

Super stats

Scientific name: Tapirus indicus
Life span: Up to 30 years
Length: 6-8¼ ft (1.8-2.5 m)
Weight: About 720 lb (326 kg)
Diet: Aquatic plants, leaves, twigs, shoots, buds, fallen fruit
Habitat: Forests and swamps
Location: Sumatra, Malaysia, southern Thailand, and Myanmar

Large white patch on black body

Long, trunklike snout

Three toes on back feet and four on front feet

Weird but true!
Tapirs can swim underwater! They curve their snouts up above the water, like snorkels.

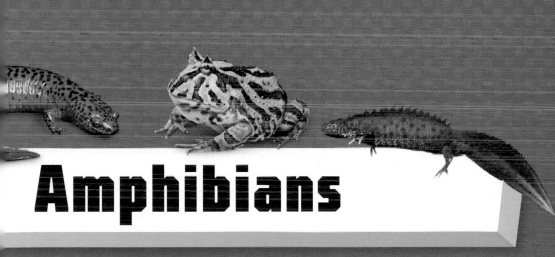

Amphibians

Amphibians are found in most parts of the world. They usually prefer soggy habitats with plenty of freshwater, such as rain forests and woods. Amphibians have wet skin, lay eggs, are cold-blooded, and have water-living young. Most of them are small and unthreatening, so they'd rather hop or swim away from danger than stay and fight. However, a few amphibians are deadly dangerous! Rain forest-living tree frogs are among the most poisonous animals on Earth.

What is an amphibian?

Water is crucial for amphibians – they spend most of their time in or near it, at every stage of their lives. But that's not all there is to it. What makes an amphibian an amphibian?

There are around 8,250 different species of amphibian.

Inner skeleton

Amphibians are vertebrates – they have a hard skeleton inside their bodies, which is made of bone.

Wet skin

Amphibian skin is smooth, thin, and wet. Most amphibians live in wet places, so that their skin does not dry out.

Egg laying

Most amphibians lay eggs, in water or in damp places on land. The eggs are covered in a jelly-like substance that feeds the babies inside.

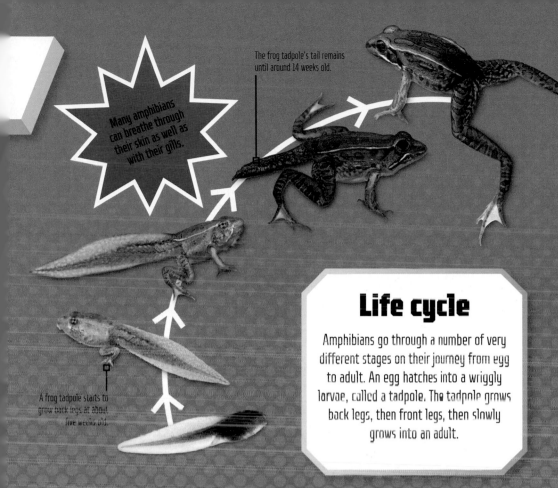

Many amphibians can breathe through their skin as well as with their gills.

The frog tadpole's tail remains until around 14 weeks old.

A frog tadpole starts to grow back legs at about five weeks old.

Life cycle

Amphibians go through a number of very different stages on their journey from egg to adult. An egg hatches into a wriggly larvae, called a tadpole. The tadpole grows back legs, then front legs, then slowly grows into an adult.

Cold blood

All amphibians have cold blood, which means their bodies are the same temperature as their surroundings. They must use the Sun's heat to get warm.

Water living

Most amphibians live in the water when they are young, taking in oxygen from it using organs called gills.

Axolotl

This salamander never really grows up, it just gets bigger. Unlike other amphibians, the axolotl keeps its gills instead of developing lungs, and spends its whole life in the water. The axolotl is only found in two lakes in Mexico.

Weird but true!
If they get hurt, axolotls can regrow their body parts —including their brain!

Feathery gills, used for breathing underwater

Simple limbs with long, thin fingers

Super stats

Scientific name: Ambystoma mexicanum
Life span: Up to 15 years
Length: 6-18 in (15-45 cm)   **Weight:** 2-8 oz (60-225 g)
Diet: Mollusks, worms, insect young, crustaceans, and fish
Habitat: Lakes   **Location:** Mexico

In the wild, axolotls are gray, green, or black. In captivity, they are often pale pink.

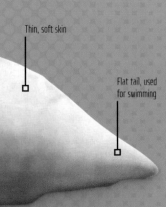

Thin, soft skin

Flat tail, used for swimming

Green tree frog

Hunting is easy for this frog as it can snap up insects that are attracted to its bright color. It lives in plants around the edges of water bodies, such as ponds and streams.

Long, strong back legs

Great crested newt

This warty newt spends most of its time on land, but returns to water to breed. The male performs a complicated dance to try to attract a female.

Crest along back, which gets taller in the breeding season

Yellow or orange belly with black blotches

Plain green back, perfect for tree camouflage

Light-colored streak along the side

Super stats

Scientific name: Dryophytes cinereus
Life span: Up to 5 years
Length: 2½ in (6 cm) **Weight:** 0.1–0.6 oz (2–17 g)
Diet: Flies, mosquitoes, and other small insects, such as crickets
Habitat: Ponds, lakes, marshes, and streams
Location: Central and southeastern USA

Weird but true!

Males make a sound like a loud quack, both to attract females and when it rains!

Weird but true!

The female great crested newt wraps each of her eggs up in a leaf.

Super stats

Scientific name: Triturus cristatus
Life span: Up to 25 years
Weight: ¼–3/8 oz (6.2–10.5 g)
Length: Up to 6¼ in (16 cm)
Diet: Worms, slugs, and insects on land, and tadpoles and mollusks in water
Habitat: Large ponds
Location: Northern Europe

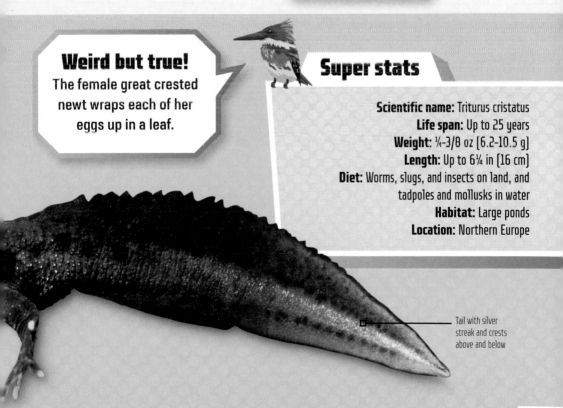

Tail with silver streak and crests above and below

Argentine horned frog

If danger looms, this frog swells its body up, making it look big and hard to attack. It then screams at the top of its voice, to try to frighten away the threat.

Weird but true!
This frog eats mainly other frogs, and even smaller frogs of the same species.

Eyes sticking up above the head

Green-and-brown splotched skin pattern

Enormous mouth, for swallowing large prey

Super stats

Scientific name: Ceratophrys ornate
Life span: 6-7 years
Length: Up to 6½ in (16.5 cm)   **Weight:** ¾-1 1/8 lb (320-480 g)
Diet: Rodents, such as mice, small reptiles, large spiders, and insects, such as locusts
Habitat: Rainforest   **Location:** Argentina, Brazil, and Uruguay

Mandarin salamander

In dry periods and during winter, this bumpy-bodied salamander spends spends most of the day hiding underground. It comes out at night to hunt insects.

Super stats

Scientific name: Tylototriton shanjing
Life span: Unknown in the wild, up to 20 years in captivity
Length: About 20 in (17 cm)
Weight: Unknown
Diet: Small invertebrates
Habitat: Pools and slow-moving streams in subtropical forests
Location: China

Warty bumps along the back

Flat, V-shaped head

Orange ridge running all the way along the body and joining up with the tail

Weird but true!

The bumps on this salamander's back aren't just for show—they show the position of glands that secrete poison.

Golden poison frog

This little frog is only about the size of a thumb, but it is extremely dangerous. In fact, it is so poisonous that a human can die just from touching its skin. It has about 20 times more poison than other South American frogs.

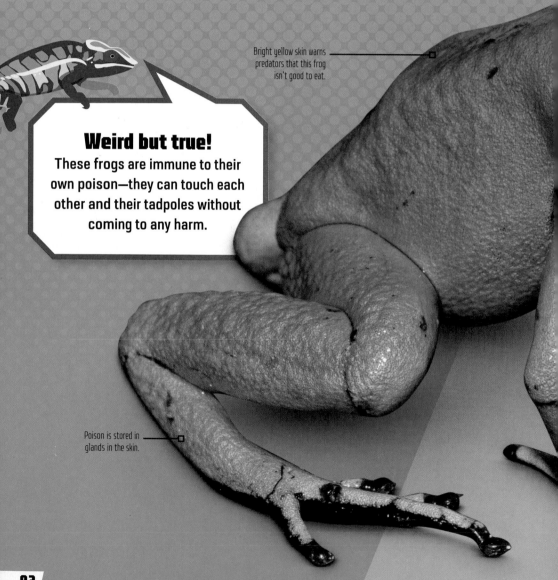

Bright yellow skin warns predators that this frog isn't good to eat.

Weird but true!
These frogs are immune to their own poison—they can touch each other and their tadpoles without coming to any harm.

Poison is stored in glands in the skin.

Super stats

Scientific name: Phyllobates terribilis
Life span: About 10 years
Length: Up to 1 in (2½ cm)   **Weight:** Less than 1 oz (28 g)
Diet: Invertebrates, such as beetles, mites, and ants
Habitat: Rain forests
Location: Mountains of western Colombia

Large black eyes

This frog's skin can be bright yellow, orange, or light green.

Wallace's flying frog

To travel between trees, this frog spreads out its feet and the flaps of skin that run along the sides of its body, then throws itself into the air. It can travel more than 50 ft (15 m) in a single leap.

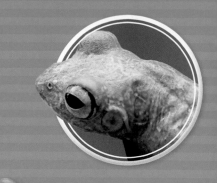

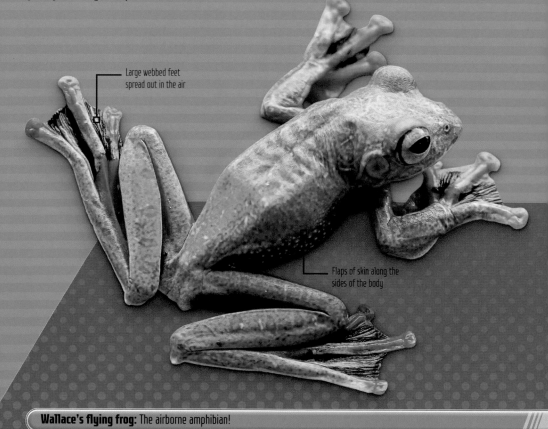

Large webbed feet spread out in the air

Flaps of skin along the sides of the body

Wallace's flying frog: The airborne amphibian!

Head-to-head!

They may appear to fly, but these two animals actually glide—they soar smoothly through the air while barely moving their muscles. So, which of them can glide the farthest?

Sunda colugo

Colugos have a huge area of skin that extends all the way to the ends of their legs and tail. When they leap into the air, this skin acts like a parachute, allowing them to glide up to 330 ft (100 m), without losing much height.

Colugos can glide as fast as some birds fly, without having wings to flap!

Skin "parachute" connecting the neck, legs, and tail

Webbing between the toes

Sunda colugo: The parachuting mammal!

Who would win?

The frog glides well, but it is smaller than the colugo, and has a smaller surface area of skin to spread out in the air. Ultimately, the colugo can glide around six times farther than the frog.

Winner!

Red salamander

If attacked, this salamander uses a distraction technique—it curls up into a ball, then waves its tail around in the air. The aim is to keep attention away from its head.

Bright red body with small black spots

Red eyes

Wet skin

long red tail

Weird but true!
This salamander lives on land in the summer and in water in the winter.

Super stats

Scientific name: Pseudotriton ruber
Life span: Up to 13 years
Length: 4-6 in (11-15 cm)   **Weight:** Unknown
Diet: smaller salamanders and invertebrates
Habitat: Streams and wooded areas under rocks, bark and leaf litter
Location: Eastern North America

White's tree frog

This frog spends its days hiding from the heat of the Sun. It often hides in human-made structures such as water barrels and bathrooms.

Sticky toe pads on each toe

Bright green skin

Weird but true!

These frogs hide in damp places such as tree hollows to keep from drying out.

Large fold of skin over the eyes

Super stats

Scientific name: Litoria caerulea   **Life span:** About 16 years
Weight: About 1¾ oz (51 g)   **Length:** 3-4½ in (7-11.5 cm)
Diet: Insects, such as moths and locusts   **Habitat:** Forests
Location: Australia, southern New Guinea, and New Zealand

California newt

This little newt is toxic—both its skin and flesh are highly poisonous due to a chemical it produces from its skin. Predators beware!

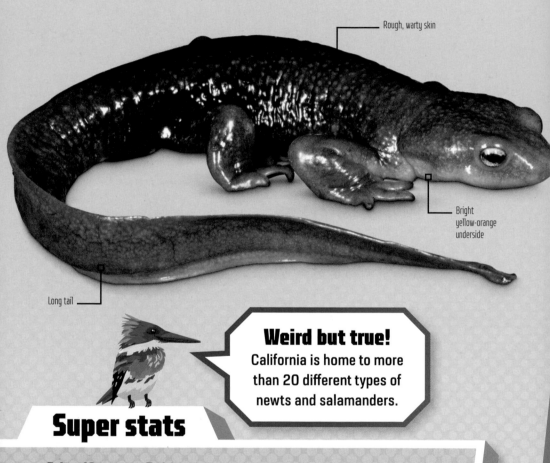

Rough, warty skin

Bright yellow-orange underside

Long tail

Weird but true!
California is home to more than 20 different types of newts and salamanders.

Super stats

Scientific name: Taricha torosa
Life span: Unknown
Weight: Unknown   **Length:** 5-8 in (12-20 cm)
Diet: Small invertebrates, such as worms and insects
Habitat: Springs and seeps that flow through fields, and woods
Location: California, USA

Tomato frog

The bright color of this frog's body warns predators that it is not good to eat. The poison its skin secretes can cause swellings and rashes in humans.

Weird but true!
Female tomato frogs are much larger and more brightly colored than males.

Smooth orange skin

Wide, round body

Long fingers on the front feet

Super stats

Scientific name: Dyscophus antongilii
Life span: More than 7 years
Length: 2¼-4¼ in (6-10.5 cm)   **Weight:** 1½-8 oz (42-226 g)
Diet: Insects, insect larvae, and worms
Habitat: Rainforest, woods, and ditches and drains in urban areas
Location: Northern Madagascar

Chinese giant salamander

This colossal creature is the world's largest amphibian. It can reach up to 6 ft (1.8 m) long—that's longer than four adult cats placed nose to tail. It spends its whole life in water, walking along river beds in search of fish and shellfish.

This salamander's skin blends in with rocks at the bottom of the water, so predators and prey don't spot it.

Gray or brown skin

Short legs stick out to the sides

Super stats

Tiny eyes

Weird but true!
Giant salamanders have hardly changed in the last 30 million years, and are sometimes called "living fossils."

Striped rocket frog

All frogs have stretchy tissue called cartilage in their toes, but this frog has extra-long cartilage, which allows it to leap farther than most. It has one of the longest leaps of all frog species, reaching an incredible 36 times its body length.

Black stripe along the sides of the head

Large, long, muscled back legs

Striped rocket frog: The stretchy-toed leaper!

Head-to-head!

These competitors are both from Australia. Strong legs and powerful muscles make them excellent at springing through the air, but which of them can make the longest jump?

Red kangaroo

This massive mammal has back legs that work like springs, propelling it up to 30 ft (9 m) in a single leap. It can bounce along at top speeds of 30 mph (50 kph)—faster than the fastest human sprinter.

Australia is home to more than 11.5 million red kangaroos.

Powerful back legs with big feet

Long tail helps the kangaroo stay balanced

Red kangaroo: The springy jumper!

Who would win?

The kangaroo can leap farther in distance—30 ft (9 m) compared to the frog's 6.5 ft (2 m)—but not compared to its size! The frog can jump 36 times its length, but the kangaroo can only jump three times its length. So, it depends!

You decide!

Leapfrog

Strong, stretchy leg muscles let some frogs make impressive leaps. Many of them can jump 10 or 20 times farther than their body's length. Not all frogs leap—some crawl or walk, and a few are able to glide in the air between trees.

European fire salamander

Bright yellow markings tell hungry predators that this salamander would be a deadly dinner. They are a warning sign that its skin is covered in poison.

Weird but true!
This salamander doesn't just ooze poison—it can also spray it at attackers from pores in its tail.

Thick tail

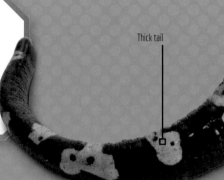

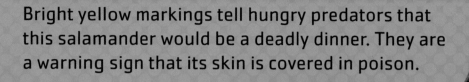

Yellow-banded frog

Tiny but dangerous, poison dart frogs are some of the most toxic animals on Earth. They become poisonous by eating ants and other animals containing toxic chemicals.

Black eyes

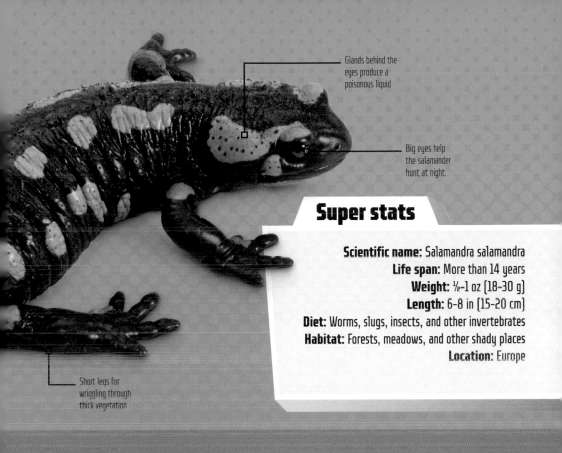

Glands behind the eyes produce a poisonous liquid

Big eyes help the salamander hunt at night.

Short legs for wriggling through thick vegetation

Super stats

Scientific name: Salamandra salamandra
Life span: More than 14 years
Weight: ½-1 oz (18-30 g)
Length: 6-8 in (15-20 cm)
Diet: Worms, slugs, insects, and other invertebrates
Habitat: Forests, meadows, and other shady places
Location: Europe

Weird but true!

Poison dart frogs come with a range of colors and markings—there are more than 120 species!

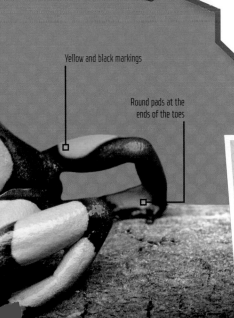

Yellow and black markings

Round pads at the ends of the toes

Super stats

Scientific name: Dendrobates leucomelas
Life span: 5-7 years
Weight: About 1/8 oz (3 g)   **Length:** 1¼-1½ in (3-4 cm)
Diet: Small insects, such as ants, termites, beetles, and crickets, and spiders
Habitat: Lowland rain forest
Location: South America

Red-eyed tree frog

This frog spends its time high up among the wet leaves of rain forest trees. Females lay their eggs on leaves that overhang water. When the eggs hatch, the tadpoles drop down into the water below.

Orange feet

Weird but true!
This frog's eggs usually hatch after around 10 days, but they can hatch early if they are in danger of being eaten!

Red eyes with vertical slit pupils

Blue and yellow patches on the sides

Super stats

Scientific name: Agalychnis callidryas
Life span: About 5 years
Length: 1½–2¾ in (3.8–6.9 cm)   **Weight:** ¼–½ oz (5.6–14.1 g)
Diet: Crickets, flies, and moths
Habitat: Rain forest   **Location:** Mexico, throughout Central America, and in northern South America

Wood frog

Freezing temperatures are no problem for this frog. When temperatures drop it freezes completely solid. Its breathing stops, and its heart no longer beats. Then, when the weather is warmer again, the frog thaws out and hops off, unharmed.

Weird but true!
Wood frogs can freeze and then thaw out again several times in the same winter.

Large brown eyes

Dark patch behind the eyes

Skin can be pink, brown, or black.

Super stats

Scientific name: Lithobates sylvaticus
Life span: Up to 4 years
Length: 1½–3¼ in (3.5-8 cm)   **Weight:** ¼ oz (7.8 g)
Diet: Insects, arachnids, worms, slugs, and snails
Habitat: Woodland   **Location:** Canada and eastern USA

Skilled defenders

Many animals have developed clever ways to avoid being eaten. Some animals use their amazing camouflage abilities to hide, while others change their appearance to make themselves seem more scary or less tasty. Some use noise to put off predators, while others just make sure that they taste really bad.

Bird-dropping spider

This spider has the ultimate unappetising disguise—it hopes that by looking like bird poo, no one will want to eat it.

Opossum

Opossums are great actors. When threatened they simply pretend to be dead already!

Porcupines

This animal has made itself into painful prey. Any predator that wants to take a bite will have to get past its sharp spikes first.

Poison dart frog

If the bright colors of this frog don't scare off predators, it hopes that its toxic skin will. It is one of the most poisonous animals in the world.

Pangolin

This clever mammal has two forms of defense. Its body is covered in hard scales that act like armor. But if the situation is really bad, it also curls up into a ball so that it is harder to grab.

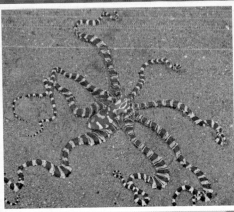

Pufferfish

These fish have several ways of putting off would-be predators. They can inflate their spiny bodies so that they look several times bigger. They also contain a toxic substance that makes them taste really bad.

Mimic octopus

The mimic octopus confuses predators by pretending to be another, less tasty, creature. It can alter its appearance to look like around 15 other sea creatures, including a lionfish, jellyfish, sea snake, sole, shrimp, and crab.

Dung beetle

Don't be put off by the dung beetle's love of poo. It is one of nature's cleaners and recyclers, rolling away dung to make a nice home or a tasty meal. And it takes some pretty big insect muscles to shift big, heavy balls of dung.

Male dung beetles also use their strength to fight each other or to win a mate.

Antennae help it locate the tastiest dung.

Strong front legs dig and collect dung.

Dung beetle: Small, helpful, and super-strong

Head-to-head!

Some big animals have amazing strength. They can lift, drag, carry or pull super-heavy things. Other animals may be tiny, but have incredible power in relation to their size. So which is stronger, an elephant or a dung beetle?

African elephant

It's no surprise that the biggest land animal is also one of the strongest. Elephants can weigh up to 140,000 lb (63,500 kg) and they can carry up to 20,000 lb (9,000 kg)—which is about the weight of 130 adult humans!

African elephants are usually heavier than Asian elephants.

Trunk has up to 100,000 muscles and can lift large trees.

Dense bones allow elephants to support their weight on their hind legs.

Elephant: Mighty land mammal

Who would win?

Although elephants can lift much heavier objects, dung beetles are proportionally stronger. They can pull around 1,141 times their own body weight, but the elephant can only lift 1.5 times its weight. In fact, the dung beetle is the strongest known animal in relation to its size.

Winner!

Mudpuppy

Flat bodies help these salamanders burrow under rocks on the riverbed. They hide there in the day, disguised by mud and silt. At night, they come out to hunt.

Weird but true!
Female mudpuppies lay up to 200 eggs, then guard them for around 40 days.

Feathery gills for breathing underwater

Olm

These salamanders live deep underground, in the watery depths of pitch black caves. They are completely blind, so they have no problem living in absolute darkness.

Weird but true!
Olms have a good sense of smell, which means they can hunt in the dark.

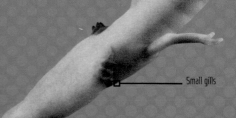

Small gills

Flattened head and body

Super stats

Scientific name: Necturus maculosus
Life span: 20 years or more
Length: 8-18 in (20-45 cm)   **Weight:** Up to 1 oz (2 g)
Diet: Crayfish, insect larvae, small fish, fish eggs, aquatic worms, snails, and other amphibians
Habitat: Streams and rivers
Location: Along the east coast of North America

Brownish skin gives camouflage on riverbeds

Long, thin body

Colorless skin

Super stats

Scientific name: Proteus anguinus
Life span: More than 100 years
Length: Up to 8 5/8 in (22 cm)   **Tail length:** Up to 3 1/8 in (8 cm).
Weight: Up to 150 g (5 1/3 oz)
Diet: Small aquatic crustaceans
Habitat: Underground waters, in limestone caves and mines
Location: Slovenia and Croatia

Mexican burrowing toad

This toad digs burrows in soft soil, then spends most of its life hidden away underground. The adult frogs only leave their burrows after there has been heavy rain. They breed, then head back underground.

Large, strong feet, for digging burrows

Surinam toad

This toad has a very unusual way of looking after its young. The fertilized eggs are placed on the female's back, which then grows around them. A few months later, fully developed toadlets break their way out.

Weird but true!
Star-shaped organs at the end of the toad's fingers help it feel for prey hidden in the mud.

Red stripe along the back

Rounded body

Small head

Super stats

Scientific name: Rhinophrynus dorsalis
Life span: Unknown
Length: 2-2¾ in (5-7 cm)   **Weight:** Unknown
Diet: Ants and termites
Habitat: Fields and plains with sandy soil
Location: Southern USA through to Costa Rica

Weird but true!

The burrowing toad can change the shape of its tongue, to catch different types of insects.

Back, where eggs develop

Strong back legs

Flat, squared-shaped body

Super stats

Scientific name: Pipa pipa
Life span: Up to 8 years
Length: 4-6 in (10-15 cm)   **Weight:** 3½-5½ oz (100-160 g)
Diet: Crustaceans, small fish, worms, and other invertebrates
Habitat: Swamps and slow-moving rivers
Location: Northern South America

Hairy frog

When it is in danger, this frog has an amazing skill—it breaks its own bones. The broken bones cut through its skin, becoming claws the frog can use to fight off attackers.

Weird but true!
The hairlike skin structures on a male hairy frog's body help it to take in oxygen.

Super stats

Scientific name: Trichobatrachus robustus
Life span: Up to 5 years
Length: 4-5 in (10-13 cm) **Weight:** Up to 3 oz (80 g)
Diet: Slugs, myriapods, spiders, beetles, and grasshoppers
Habitat: Subtropical or tropical moist lowland forests, rivers, arable land, and plantations
Location: Central Africa

Mottled brown skin

Hairlike structures on the body only appear in the breeding season

Claws on the back feet

Purple frog

This frog lives beneath the ground, and only comes out once a year in the rainy season, to breed. To attract a mate, the male makes a strange, chickenlike sound. After a few hours or days, it burrows back into the soil.

Super stats

Scientific name: Nasikabatrachus sahyadrensis
Life span: Unknown
Length: About 2¾ in [7 cm]
Weight: About 5¾ oz [165 g]
Diet: Termites
Habitat: Underground near ponds and ditches or streams
Location: Western Ghats in India

Pointed snout

Purple-brown body

Rounded body shape

Weird but true!

This frog's tadpoles cling to rocks in fast-flowing water by using their mouths as suckers.

Wallace's flying frog

To hop from one tree to the next, this frog appears to fly—it spreads its legs and toes wide and leaps into the air. It controls its flight path by gently tilting its feet as it glides, which allows it to land exactly where it wants.

Weird but true!
This frog spends most its life without touching the ground, only leaving the trees to breed.

Yellow feet

Sticky pads on the toes allow this frog to cling to leaves.

Super stats

Scientific name: Rhacophorus nigropalmatus
Life span: Unknown
Length: 3 1/8-3 7/8 in (8-10 cm)
Weight: Unknown
Diet: Insects, and other small invertebrates
Habitat: Rain forest
Location: Indonesia, Malaysia, and Thailand

Bright green body

Wide feet, with black webbing between the toes

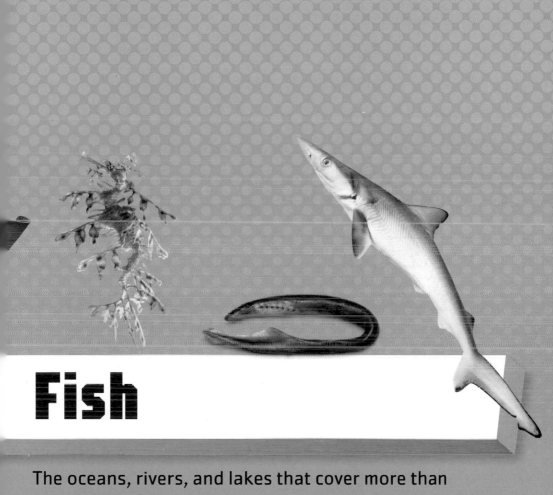

Fish

The oceans, rivers, and lakes that cover more than two-thirds of our planet are home to thousands of different types of fish. This incredible group of creatures has lived on Earth for about 500 million years. Many have adapted to their watery world by developing a streamlined shape, as well as fins and tails for swimming. They all have special slits called gills that take in oxygen to breathe underwater. Fish can be a variety of shapes, sizes, patterns, and colors, ranging from sharks the size of buses to fish that are too small to see without a microscope.

What is a fish?

There are at least 33,000 types of fish and they come in many different forms. Huge, wide-mouthed sharks are fish, and so are tiny seahorses with curled tails. But despite their differences, all fish live in water and breathe through gills.

Backbone

Dorsal fin

Tail

Operculum flap covering gills

Pectoral fins

Scales

Pelvic fins

Hot or cold?

Different types of fish tend to be found in different temperatures of water. Fish living in colder seas are usually dull in color, but in warmer, tropical water they are often brightly colored.

Fresh or salt?

Most fish live in the salty water of the oceans and seas. However, some fish inhabit freshwater lakes and rivers. The salmon is an example of a fish that can live in either habitat.

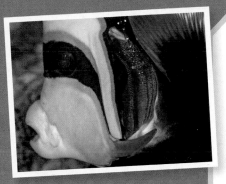

Breathing

A fish swallows water through its mouth. The water passes to the gills, which take oxygen from it for the fish to breathe. The remaining water is filtered out from under the operculum flap.

Bony or rubbery?

Most fish have bony skeletons—95 percent of them, in fact! Sharks and a few other types of fish have softer bodies made of a rubbery tissue called cartilage.

Swimming

Fish are superb swimmers. This is partly because of their fins—a dorsal fin at the top keeps the fish stable and upright in water, the pectoral fins help with turning, and pelvic fins are used to change direction. A tail full of muscles helps propel the fish forward.

Scales

Many fish are covered in hundreds of waterproof scales. This shiny, slimy layer helps them to move easily through the water.

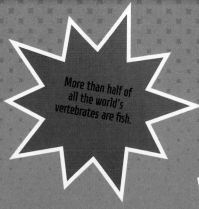

More than half of all the world's vertebrates are fish.

Life on the reef

The Great Barrier Reef is the largest coral reef on Earth, spanning 132,900 sq miles (344,400 sq km) off the coast of Australia. Reefs look rocky, but colorful coral is really the skeletons of masses of tiny sea creatures, built up over time. More than 1,500 types of fish live here, enjoying the warm temperatures, safe shelter, and plentiful food, such as plants.

Spiny dogfish

This small shark swims at high speed through Pacific and Atlantic waters, keeping alert for attacks. If a predatory shark or whale comes too close, the spiny dogfish arches its back and injects toxic venom from two sharp spines.

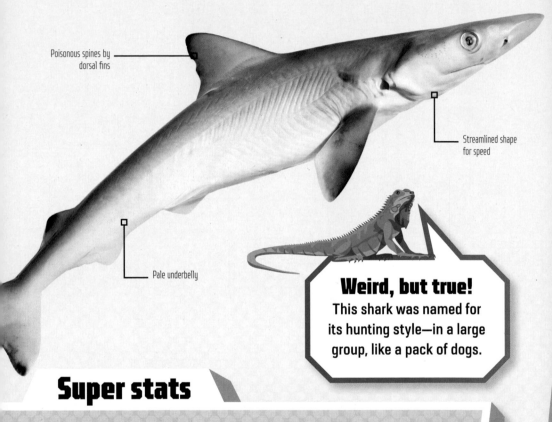

Poisonous spines by dorsal fins

Streamlined shape for speed

Pale underbelly

Weird, but true!
This shark was named for its hunting style—in a large group, like a pack of dogs.

Super stats

Scientific name: Squalus acanthias
Life span: 35-40 years
Length: Up to 4 ft (1.2 m) **Weight:** 8 lb (3.6 kg)
Diet: Small fish, such as herring, and invertebrates, such as crabs
Habitat: Ocean, usually temperate or subarctic
Location: North Atlantic and North Pacific oceans

Anglerfish

The darkest depths of the ocean are lit up by female anglerfish. They have a natural light hanging from their heads to attract prey. Fish take the bait, like a fishing line. They swim toward the only glow in the gloom and get swallowed up whole.

Weird, but true!
The mouth of the anglerfish can open wide to swallow prey double its size.

Dangling light shining in the darkness

Jagged teeth inside the gaping mouth

Small fins allow for slow, wobbly swimming

Super stats

Scientific name: Lophiiformes
Life span: Up to 25 years
Length: 8-40 in (20-100 cm)   **Weight:** Up to 110 lb (50 kg)
Diet: Fish and invertebrates
Habitat: Ocean, to depths of 3,300 ft (1,000 m)
Location: Atlantic and Antarctic oceans

Spotted eagle ray

A spotted pattern and giant, winglike fins inspired this ray's name. It is a superb swimmer, thanks to the size of its fins. If predators come too close, the ray hits back with its powerful, stinging tail!

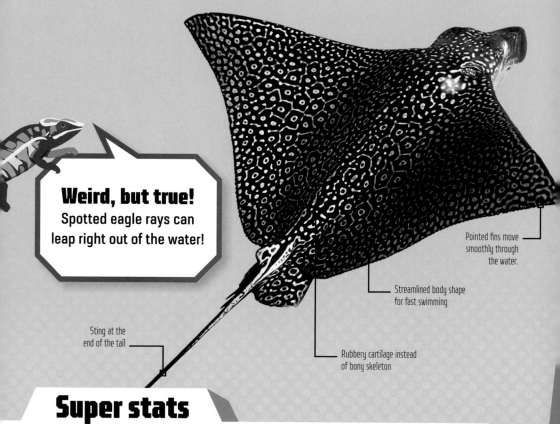

Weird, but true!
Spotted eagle rays can leap right out of the water!

Pointed fins move smoothly through the water.

Streamlined body shape for fast swimming

Sting at the end of the tail

Rubbery cartilage instead of bony skeleton

Super stats

Scientific name: Aetobatus narinari
Life span: Up to 20 years
Length: Up to 16 ft (5 m)   **Weight:** Around 500 lb (230 kg)
Diet: Mollusks, crabs, octopuses, small fish, and worms
Habitat: Tropical coastal waters **Location:** Indo-Pacific and Eastern and Western Atlantic oceans

Bennett's flying fish

This fish can break through the surface of tropical seas to soar through the air. It can travel at airborne speeds of up to 10 mph (16 km/h hour), away from ocean predators. Back underwater it survives by munching away on tiny plankton.

Super stats

Scientific name: Cheilopogon pinnatibarbatus
Life span: Up to 5 years
Length: Up to 19 in (48 cm)
Weight: Up to 2 lb (0.9 kg)
Diet: Zooplankton and small fish
Habitat: Near shore waters
Location: Worldwide in tropic and subtropical water

Bullet-shaped body

Four fins spread out for fast flight.

Forked tail suited to swimming

Weird, but true!
Flying fish can remain airborne for 30 seconds at a time.

Red-bellied piranha

This fish swims through the rivers of South America in search of insects and fish, before ripping them apart with razor-sharp teeth. To stay safe from the snapping jaws of caiman and predatory birds, it swims in a large group.

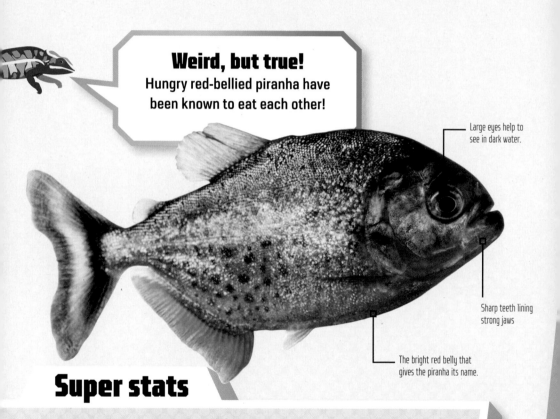

Weird, but true!
Hungry red-bellied piranha have been known to eat each other!

Large eyes help to see in dark water.

Sharp teeth lining strong jaws

The bright red belly that gives the piranha its name.

Super stats

Scientific name: Pygocentrus nattereri
Life span: 10 years or more
Length: 12 in (30 cm)   **Weight:** 4 lb (1.8 kg)
Diet: Bits of flesh, small fish, insects, invertebrates, and sometimes fruit
Habitat: Lakes and rivers   **Location:** Amazon River basin, South America

Leafy sea dragon

Related to seahorses, leafy sea dragons have an unusual, frilly form. Swaying slowly, they look just like seaweed floating in the water. Predators swim past without noticing, and so do shrimp and other prey.

Long snout used for feeding

Colors provide camouflage against rocks and seagrasses.

Frilly flaps floating in the water

Weird, but true!

Unlike most females in the animal kingdom, female sea dragons leave their eggs in the pouches of male sea dragons for them to care for.

Super stats

Scientific name: Phycodurus eques
Life span: Unknown in the wild
Length: 12 in (30 cm)   **Weight:** 3½ oz (100 g)
Diet: Shrimp, sea lice
Habitat: Reefs and seagrass beds   **Location:** Eastern Indian Ocean and along the southern coast of Australia

Atlantic mudskipper

This unusual fish can live out of water! The Atlantic mudskipper pulls itself along on land using the fins like powerful arms, but it can also jump and climb. Crawling along shores and through swamps, it hunts small prey.

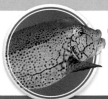

Yellow boxfish

Boxfish are protected by the ultimate body armor. Instead of scales, they have a covering of thick bony plates that stops predators from eating them. This form of defense allows very limited movement, so boxfish must beat their fins extra hard to swim through the water.

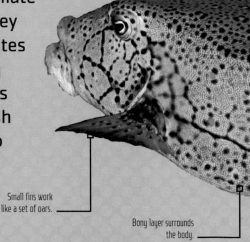

Small fins work like a set of oars.

Bony layer surrounds the body.

Eyes can see clearly in both water and air.

Mouth and skin take in oxygen to breathe.

Weird, but true!

Mudskippers can stay on land for 90 percent of their lives.

Fins are designed to move on land.

Super stats

Scientific name: Periophthalmus barbarus
Life span: Up to 5 years
Length: 3-10 in (7.5-25 cm)
Weight: 0.02-2 oz (0.5-65 g)
Diet: Invertebrates, fish, and crustaceans **Habitat:** Estuaries, lagoons, and mangrove swamps **Location:** Western Africa coastline

Weird, but true!

Some boxfish also release poisonous slime from their skin to scare predators.

Super stats

Scientific name: Ostracion cubicus
Life span: Around 4 years
Length: Up to 18 in (45 cm) **Weight:** 3½ lb (1.5 kg)
Diet: Mollusks, crustaceans, fish, worms, and algae
Habitat: Coral and rocky reefs
Location: Indo-West Pacific

Big tail helps with swimming and steering.

Red lionfish

Super stats

Scientific name: Pterois volitans
Life span: Up to 15 years
Length: 8-15 in (20-38 cm)
Weight: Up to 2½ lb (1.1 kg)   **Diet:** Fish, crabs, shrimp, snails, and other small marine animals   **Habitat:** Rocky outcrops, coral reefs, muddy waters, and lagoons
Location: Tropical coastlines from the Indian Ocean to the central Pacific Ocean

Although they're a lot smaller than lions on land, lionfish are also deadly predators. Those spectacular spines are packed with poison and sting any attackers in the tropical waters where they live.

Weird, but true!
The poisonous spines of the lionfish are powerful enough to paralyze people.

Long poisonous spines along the back

Deadly fins contain sharp spines.

Red-and-white stripes warn predators to stay away.

Green parrotfish

Parrotfish share their strong beaks and bright colors with parrots. They use their beaks to break off coral and crunch it up to eat the algae attached to it. The swallowed coral gets ground down and pooped out as sand!

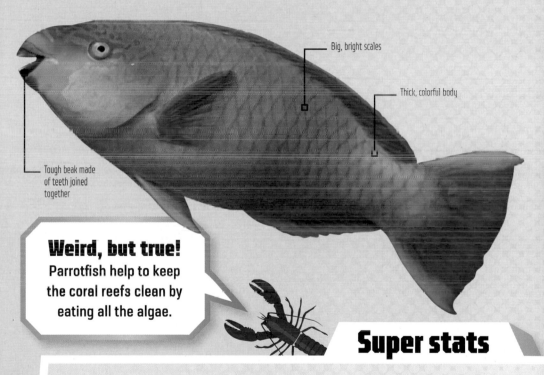

Big, bright scales

Thick, colorful body

Tough beak made of teeth joined together

Weird, but true!
Parrotfish help to keep the coral reefs clean by eating all the algae.

Super stats

Scientific name: Scarus quoyi
Life span: Up to 7 years
Length: 12–20 in (30–50 cm) **Weight:** Up to 165 lb (75 kg)
Diet: Algae **Habitat:** Shallow ocean waters and coral reefs
Location: Worldwide, but especially in the tropics

Sea lamprey

Beware this sea sucker! A sea lamprey's mouth is a superstrong suction device that it attaches to prey. This creates a hole in the prey's skin, used to suck out flesh and blood. Only fully grown sea lamprey live in the sea—fish eggs are laid in rivers, where baby fish stay.

Weird, but true!
Sea lampreys are also called vampire fish because of their sucking style of attack.

Long, sleek body like an eel

Gill slits for breathing on the outside

Two dorsal fins along the back

Super stats

Scientific name: Petromyzon marinus
Life span: Up to 5 years
Length: Up to 4 ft (1.2 m)   **Weight:** Up to 5½ lb (2.5 kg)
Diet: Fish   **Habitat:** They live in oceans, and spawn (lay eggs) in freshwater
Location: Rivers and coasts of Europe and North America

Long-spine porcupinefish

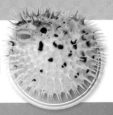

If a predator is near, this fish transforms its size and shape. Gulping down lots of water allows it to blow up like a beach ball, and the flattened spines that cover its body stand out. It's now too big and spiked to swallow!

Sharp spines are used for self-defense.

Large eyes watch out for predators.

Weird, but true!
Porcupinefish are a type of pufferfish—a whole family of inflatable fish!

Ball-shaped body inflated with water

Super stats

Scientific name: Diodon hystrix
Life span: Unknown
Length: Around 6 in [15 cm]   **Weight:** Unknown
Diet: Shellfish, such as hermit crabs, limpets, periwinkles, and whelks
Habitat: Shallow ocean areas, such as coral reefs
Location: Worldwide

Sydney funnel-web spider

Native to Australia, the Sydney funnel-web is one of the world's deadliest spiders. Under threat, it rears up on its back legs, shows its fangs, and gives a deadly bite. The toxic venom is powerful enough to kill and leaves fang marks like a vampire bite!

This spider's giant fangs are larger than some snake fangs!

Dark, shiny body

Biting fangs

Long, fast legs

Sydney funnel-web spider: Eight-legged attacker

Head-to-head!

Some creatures come equipped with deadly venom. If they feel threatened, or if they are hunting prey, they can unleash this secret weapon to kill. But who is the most deadly of these two venomous creatures?

Reef stonefish

Watch out for the reef stonefish! This is one of the most venomous fish on Earth. It lies low on coral reefs and changes color to blend in with the sand and rock. But if the reef stonefish is disturbed, it fights back. The sharp spines release powerful venom with devastating effect.

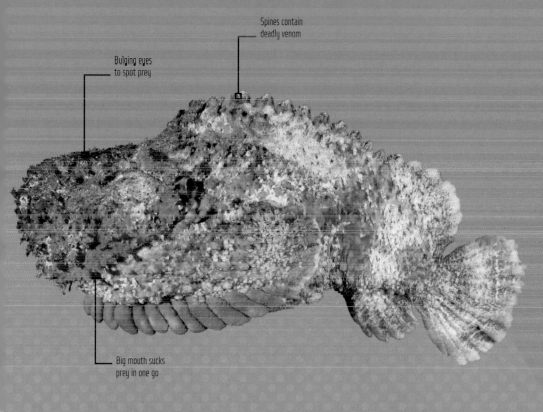

Spines contain
deadly venom

Bulging eyes
to spot prey

Big mouth sucks
prey in one go

Reef stonefish: The deadliest rock

Who would win?

Someone injected with stonefish venom would die within hours, while someone bitten by a funnel-web spider could live for up to three days. The stonefish is the winner—but immediate hospital treatment with antivenom offers a good chance of survival from both species. Phew!

Winner!

Tassled scorpion fish

This master of disguise uses the coral reefs as camouflage. It changes color to suit its surroundings, while tassels of skin blend in with seaweed and seagrass. The tassled scorpion fish stays on the seabed, waiting to swallow passing fish and crustaceans.

Giant manta ray

The undisputed king of the rays is the giant manta ray, with an average wingspan of 26 ft (8 m)—the same length as a double-decker bus! This gentle giant moves through the water slowly and calmly while feeding on huge amounts of tiny sea creatures, called zooplankton.

Enormous flapping fins

Skin has no scales

Venomous spines can rise up along the back.

Colors match the reefs and rocks.

Skin tassels hanging from the jaw

Super stats

Scientific name: Scorpaenopsis oxycephala
Life span: About 15 years
Length: Up to 14 in (36 cm)
Weight: Up to 3½ lb (1.5 kg)
Diet: Small fish, crustaceans, and snails
Habitat: Marine; clear-water outer reef slopes and channels   **Location:** Parts of the Indo-West Pacific Ocean

Weird, but true!
The tassled scorpion fish Is one of the world's most venomous fish.

Gill slits open on the outside

Super stats

Scientific name: Manta birostris
Life span: Up to 40 years
Length: Up to 30 ft (9 m)
Weight: Up to 5,300 lb (2,400 kg)
Diet: Zooplankton   **Habitat:** Near coral and rocky reefs and in open ocean
Location: Atlantic Ocean, Pacific Ocean, and Indian Ocean

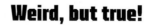

Weird, but true!
Giant Manta Rays' wingspans can reach up to 30 ft (9 m)!

Reef stonefish

When a reef stonefish is under threat, its sharp spines release deadly poison to kill predators. This stonelike fish can also change color to camouflage itself against sand and rocks on the ocean floor, so that passing prey are caught unaware.

Weird, but true!
The stonefish can swallow prey in one bite.

Colors merge with the seabed.

Dorsal spines contain powerful poison.

Bulging eyes can spot nearby prey.

Powerful mouth sucks down prey.

Super stats

Scientific name: Synanceia verrucosa
Life span: 5–10 years
Length: Up to 24 in (60 cm)   **Weight:** About 5 lb (2 kg)
Diet: Fish and crustaceans   **Habitat:** Coral bottoms
Location: Indo-Pacific Ocean

Flathead catfish

The catfish is easy to identify because it has long barbels, which are spines that look like a cat's whiskers. In murky water, a catfish relies on its barbels to taste and smell approaching prey. It swims at high speed before clutching the fish and swallowing it whole.

Super stats

Scientific name: Pylodictis olivaris
Life span: Up to 20 years
Length: 25-46 in (64-117 cm)
Weight: Up to 123 lb (56 kg)
Diet: Fish, including bass, bream, crayfish, and other catfish
Habitat: Rivers
Location: North America

Long, sleek body

Strong fins for speedy swimming

Sensitive barbels grow on the nose, mouth, and chin.

Large mouth without any teeth

Weird, but true!
Catfish live in the waters of every continent except Antarctica.

Long-snouted seahorse

This unusual fish has a head like a horse and a curly tail. Among the ocean's slowest movers, the seahorse swims in an upright position and gets around by beating its small back fin. It stays in one place by wrapping its long tail around marine plants.

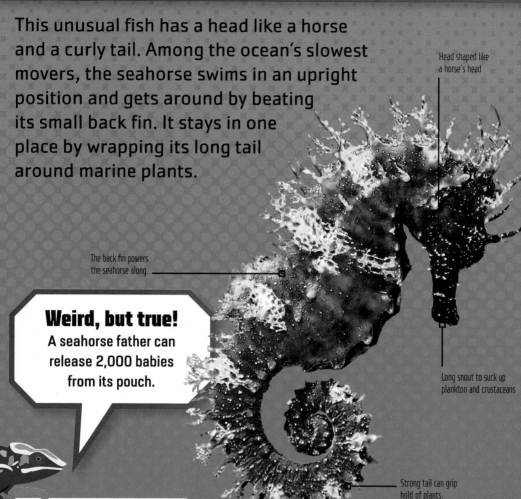

Head shaped like a horse's head

The back fin powers the seahorse along.

Weird, but true!
A seahorse father can release 2,000 babies from its pouch.

Long snout to suck up plankton and crustaceans

Strong tail can grip hold of plants.

Super stats

Scientific name: Hippocampus guttulatus
Life span: 1–5 years
Weight: Unknown   **Length:** Up to 6 in (15 cm)
Diet: Tiny swimming animals, such as copepods and plankton   **Habitat:** Shallow coastal ocean waters
Location: Atlantic coast, from the UK to the Mediterranean Sea

Neon tetra

Although only the size of a paper clip, this fish stands out in murky river water because of its shining red stripes. A friendly fish, the neon tetra loves swimming in schools for both company and safety.

Weird, but true!
Neon tetra are kept as pets in millions of fish tanks around the world.

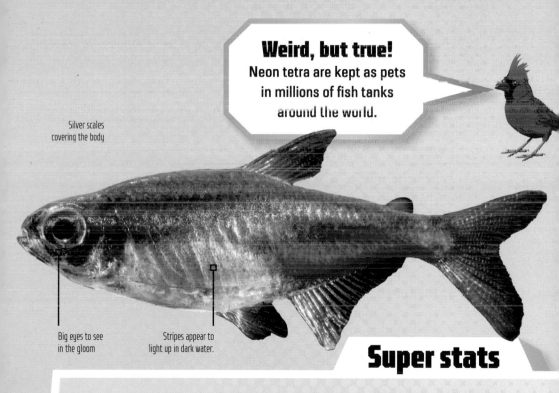

Silver scales covering the body

Big eyes to see in the gloom

Stripes appear to light up in dark water.

Super stats

Scientific name: Paracheirodon innesi
Life span: Up to 10 years
Weight: Around 0.007 oz (200 mg) **Length:** About 1½ in (4 cm)
Diet: Algae, small insects, and insect larvae
Habitat: Freshwater streams and rivers
Location: The Amazon River basin in South America

Cownose ray

The cownose ray is named for its unique head shape, which looks like the nose of a cow. This skillful swimmer flaps its fins to travel long distances through the oceans. It takes any opportunity to hunt down clams, crabs, and sea snails along the way.

Fins work like wings in the water.

The head is the same shape as a cow's nose.

Sting in the tail

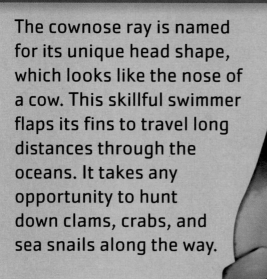

Weird, but true!
Huge groups of up to 10,000 cownose rays have been spotted traveling together.

Super stats

Scientific name: Rhinoptera bonasus
Life span: 15-20 years
Length: 24-32 in (60-78 cm)   **Weight:** Up to 50 lb (23 kg)
Diet: Small marine animals, including mollusks, bony fish, and bivalves, such as clams   **Habitat:** Ocean and brackish waters, estuaries, and bays
Location: East and Western Atlantic Ocean and Gulf of Mexico

Giant oarfish

The world's longest bony fish, the giant oarfish can measure as long as a rowboat! Despite its super size, this ocean-dweller is peaceful and its favorite food is a tiny type of plankton, called krill. Old myths and legends about sea serpents may have been based on giant oarfish.

Weird, but true!
In Japanese legend, sighting a giant oarfish meant an earthquake was likely.

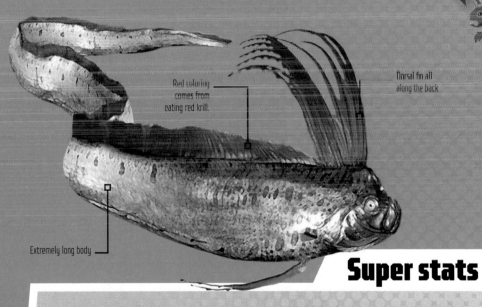

Red coloring comes from eating red krill.

Dorsal fin all along the back

Extremely long body

Super stats

Scientific name: Regalecus glesne
Life span: Unknown
Length: Up to 50 ft (15 m)   **Weight:** About 660 lb (300 kg)
Diet: Plankton, crustaceans, and squid
Habitat: Deep tropic and subtropic waters
Location: Worldwide

Betta

Weird, but true!
Fights between two bettas can continue for hours.

Also known as the Siamese fighting fish, this creature is always ready for a fight. It guards its territory in the freshwater streams and paddy fields of Southeast Asia. Battles between betta involve lots of biting and barging.

Streamlined body shape

Flowing fins

The body is around half the length of a pencil.

Super stats

Scientific name: Betta Splenden
Life span: About 2 years
Weight: Less than 1 lb [0.002 g]   **Length:** 2½ in (6 cm)
Diet: Small animals, including crustaceans, plankton, and insect larvae
Habitat: Freshwater, including marshes and other bodies of shallow water
Location: Thailand, Malaysia, Indonesia, Vietnam, Cambodia, and Laos

Orange clownfish

The clownfish has a brightly striped face that looks like a circus clown's painted face. This small fish avoids predators by living among poisonous sea anemones in the warm waters of coral reefs. Clownfish never get stung, however, because they have a protective layer of slime.

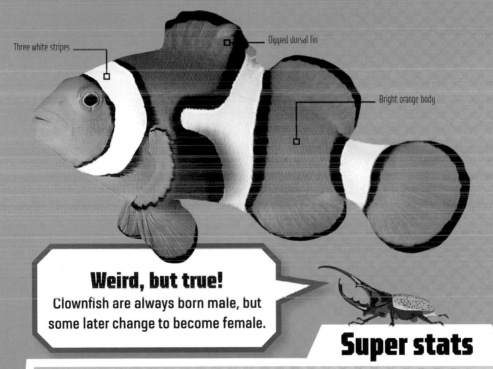

Three white stripes

Dipped dorsal fin

Bright orange body

Weird, but true!
Clownfish are always born male, but some later change to become female.

Super stats

Scientific name: Amphiprion percula   **Life span:** Up to 30 years
Weight: Around 9 oz (250 g)
Length: Around 4½ in (11 cm)
Diet: Algae, zooplankton, worms, and small crustaceans
Habitat: Coral reefs   **Location:** The Indian Ocean, the Red Sea, and the western Pacific Ocean

Australian ghost shark

Despite its name, this large fish isn't a real shark. It has a long, trunklike snout and is sometimes called the elephant fish. The sensitive snout is perfect for finding fish and shellfish to eat along the ocean floor of southern Australia.

Shiny silver skin

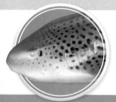

Zebra shark

Young zebra sharks have dark and light stripes, like zebras— but when they are fully grown, the stripes turn into spots. This slow-moving shark loves lazing around coral reefs by day and hunting little fish and crustaceans by night.

Whiskery barbels spread out to feel prey in the dark of night.

Black spots of adult skin

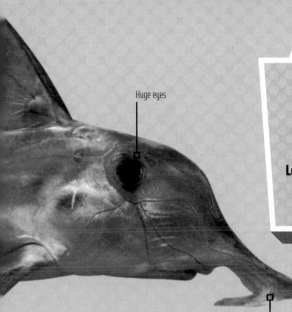

Huge eyes

The snout detects the movement of prey.

Super stats

Scientific name: Callorhinchus milii
Life span: About 15 years
Weight: Unknown   **Length:** 4 ft (1.25 m)
Diet: Shellfish and mollusks
Habitat: Continental shelves
Location: Southwestern Pacific Ocean along the coasts of southern Australia and New Zealand

Weird, but true!
Ghost sharks are ancient creatures that have lived on Earth for 400 million years.

Weird, but true!
Zebra sharks are a type of carpet shark—named so because they spend so much time resting on the seabed.

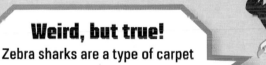

Its long, flexible body can squeeze into coral crevices.

Super stats

Scientific name: Stegostoma fasciatum
Life span: 25-30 years
Weight: 35-44 lb (16-20 kg)
Length: Up to 11.5 ft (3.5 m)
Diet: Mollusks, crustaceans, small fish, and sea snakes
Habitat: Coral reefs and rocky and sandy seabeds
Location: Indian Ocean and western Pacific Ocean

Swordfish

This huge, high-speed hunter has excellent eyesight and a bullet-shaped body to cut through the water. Its ultimate weapon is a giant sword for a snout that slices, slashes, and even knocks out prey with devastating accuracy.

Swordfish have no teeth! They use their snout to attack prey, and then swallow the prey whole.

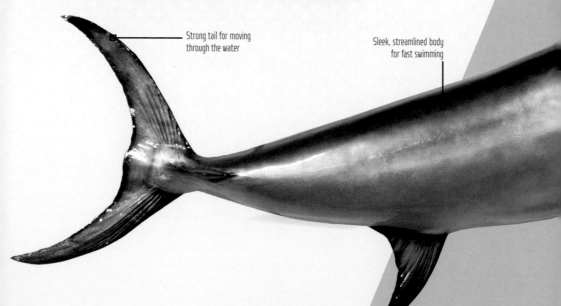

Strong tail for moving through the water

Sleek, streamlined body for fast swimming

Super stats

Scientific name: Xiphias gladius
Lifespan: About 9 years
Length: 14¾ ft (4.5 m)
Weight: About 1,165 lb (530 kg)
Diet: Fish and invertebrates, such as squid
Habitat: Oceans
Location: Atlantic, Pacific, and Indian Oceans, and the Mediterranean Sea

Pointed snout
used as a sword!

Weird but true!
The snout of the swordfish can measure 3¼ ft (1 m) long!

Cuvier's beaked whale

The Cuvier's beaked whale is a real record-breaker! Amazingly, this whale can hold its breath for more than two hours, which is longer than any other mammal. This allows it to dive deeper than any other mammal, too—it has been seen swimming just under 2 miles (3 km) underwater!

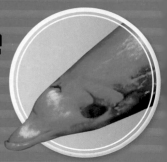

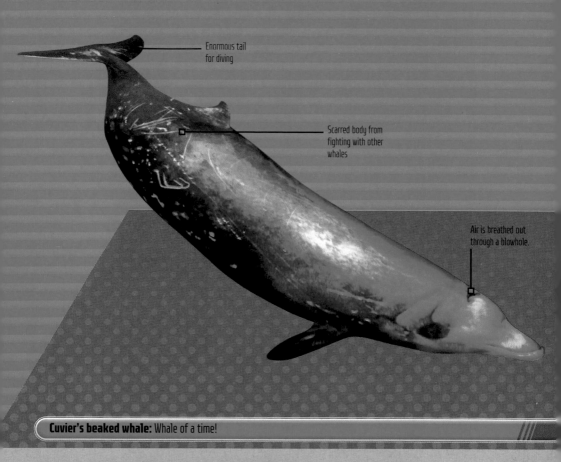

Enormous tail for diving

Scarred body from fighting with other whales

Air is breathed out through a blowhole.

Cuvier's beaked whale: Whale of a time!

Head-to-head!

Marine mammals have learned to hold their breath to dive underwater for food. But fish can breathe in water, allowing them to live deep in the ocean. So which of these two types of animal can be found at the deepest depth?

Mariana snailfish

The Mariana snailfish was found deeper in the ocean than any other fish. It lives about 5 miles (8 km) underwater in the deepest part of the Pacific Ocean, called the Mariana Trench. This strong snailfish survives despite the extreme pressure, freezing cold, and endless darkness.

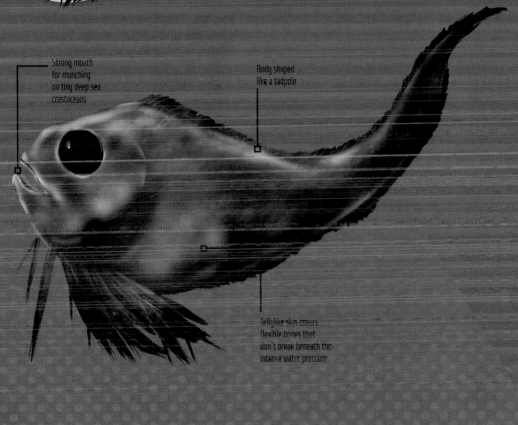

Strong mouth for munching on tiny deep sea crustaceans

Body shaped like a tadpole

Jellylike skin covers flexible bones that don't break beneath the intense water pressure

Mariana snailfish: Super snailfish

Who would win?

The winning animal doesn't have to swim up to the surface for oxygen, and it has a specially adapted body that isn't crushed under the pressure of deep, deep water. The Mariana snailfish is the deepest-dwelling creature in this competition!

Winner!

Migration

Many animals make epic journeys, called migrations, which can cross entire oceans. Some animals travel to feed or breed somewhere new. Others escape the cold by following the Sun to warmer places. Most travel in large groups to stay safe and avoid predator attacks on the way.

Start: Mississippi River
End: Up to 2,000 miles (3,200 km) away

In springtime, **American paddlefish** travel up the Mississippi River to reach deeper water. Once females find a suitable spot with the right conditions, they release their eggs. A week later, the eggs hatch and the babies are taken back downstream.

Start: Canada
End: Mexico

When it gets to the colder months in Canada, **monarch butterflies** fly to sunny Mexico. The trip can take two months to complete. After arrival, it is time for a long sleep to recover. They then lay eggs as they go north in spring. Amazingly, the new butterflies know to fly all the way back!

Start: Greenland
End: UK

Barnacle geese leave the icy chill of Greenland and head south for the winter. They fly to northern parts of the UK where the temperatures are milder. Here they spend the season grazing on green plants before flying back home in spring.

Start: Northern USA
End: Southern USA

Bottlenose dolphins prefer tropical waters. When the water temperature drops, they swim south along the Atlantic coast for the winter. More fish live in the warmer water, providing plenty of prey for the dolphins.

Psychedelic frogfish

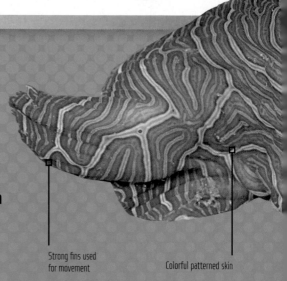

This eye-catching frogfish lives in the tropical waters of Indonesia. The contrasting colors and whirly, swirly pattern create a confusing camouflage for predators. Instead of swimming, frogfish move across the sea bed on their fins and can even hop like a frog!

Strong fins used for movement

Colorful patterned skin

X-ray fish

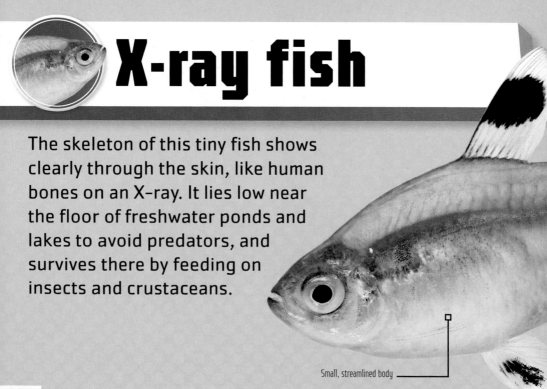

The skeleton of this tiny fish shows clearly through the skin, like human bones on an X-ray. It lies low near the floor of freshwater ponds and lakes to avoid predators, and survives there by feeding on insects and crustaceans.

Small, streamlined body

Bright blue eyes

Weird but true!
Every psychedelic
frogfish has its own
unique skin pattern.

Super stats

Scientific name: Histiophryne psychedelica
Life span: Unknown
Length: Up to 5⅞ in (15 cm)
Weight: Unknown
Diet: Shrimp and small fish
Habitat: Tropical coastal waters
Location: Waters around the islands of
Dali and Moluccas in Indonesia

Super stats

Scientific name: Pristella maxillaris
Life span: 2-5 years
Length: Up to 1⅞ in (4.8 cm)
Weight: Unknown
Diet: Small worms, insects, and crustaceans
Habitat: Freshwater ponds and lakes
Location: Amazon basin regions of Brazil, Guyana,
and Venezuela

See-through skin reveals the skeleton

Colorful, striped fins

Weird but true!
The see-through skin helps the
x-ray fish swim unnoticed
in the water.

Electric eel

Like a swimming snake, the electric eel moves slowly through the swampy waters of South America, on the hunt for food to eat. Inside its body are three electric organs that release powerful shocks used to stun or kill prey.

Long, snakelike body

European eel

European eels are born in the open ocean, but from here they go on an epic journey inland through freshwater rivers. Once they have matured, females swim long distances back to the sea to lay eggs in the same spot where they were born.

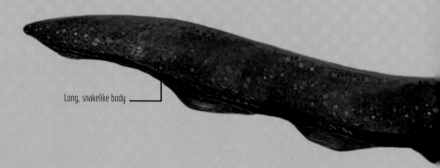

Tiny teeth inside a strong mouth

Small pair of fins

Super stats

Scientific name: Electrophorus electricus
Life span: Unknown in the wild;
up to 22 years in captivity
Length: 8 ft (2.5 m)   **Weight:** 48 lb (22 kg)
Diet: Other fish, small mammals, and inverterbrates
Habitat: Dark, muddy rivers
Location: Northern South America

Weird, but true!

The average electricity socket is 110 volts, but an electric eel produces 660 volts!

Slimy skin without scales

Big mouth to feast on
fish and crustaceans

Super stats

Scientific name: Anguilla anguilla
Life span: 5–20 years
Length: Up to 4 ft (1.3 m)   **Weight:** Up to 14 lb (6.5 kg)
Diet: Invertebrates, worms, and carrion
Habitat: Freshwater or estuaries, and the ocean
Location: Atlantic Ocean and rivers of North Atlantic,
Baltic, and Mediterranean seas. Spawning area in
western Atlantic's Sargasso Sea

Weird, but true!

The oldest European eel on record was 155 years old.

Sleek, streamlined body

Bowhead whale

The world's longest-living mammal is the bowhead whale. This survival expert can live for 200 years in Arctic waters. Despite the freezing temperatures, the bowhead whale has layers of blubber for warmth and special cells that repair themselves and prevent against deadly diseases.

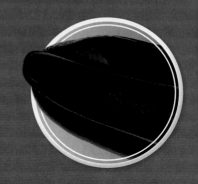

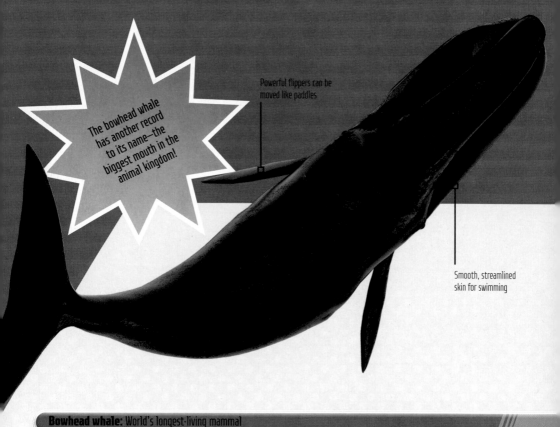

The bowhead whale has another record to its name—the biggest mouth in the animal kingdom!

Powerful flippers can be moved like paddles

Smooth, streamlined skin for swimming

Bowhead whale: World's longest-living mammal

Head-to-head!

Most people would be happy to live to 100 years old. But this is young compared to some other creatures! So who would live the longest out of the animals on this page?

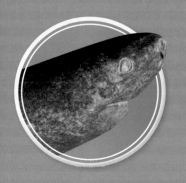

Greenland shark

This sizable shark swims slowly through the icy waters of the Atlantic Ocean on the lookout for passing prey or leftover food. Every year it grows another ⅜ in (1 cm) longer. This means the bigger the shark, the older it is—and some have been spotted measuring a whopping 16 ⅜ ft (5 m) long....

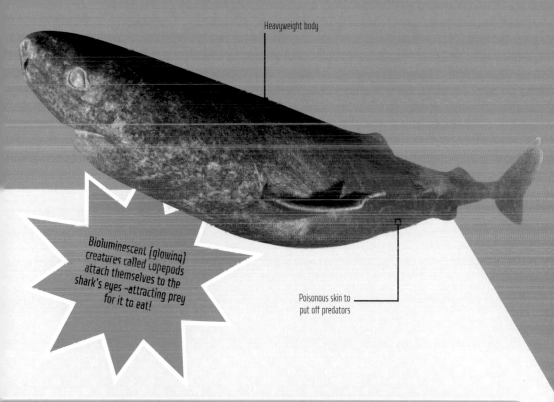

Heavyweight body

Bioluminescent (glowing) creatures called copepods attach themselves to the shark's eyes –attracting prey for it to eat!

Poisonous skin to put off predators

Greenland shark: Feisty fish

Who would win?

The oldest Greenland shark ever studied was between 272 and 512 years old—but scientists think she was probably right in the middle of these ages, at around 400. That means the greenland shark takes the crown for the world's longest-living vertebrate. Some sea sponges can live for thousands of years!

Winner!

Great white shark

This huge hunter has no natural predators to fear, which means it is at the top of the food chain. Swimming silently through the oceans, the great white seizes any opportunity to satisfy its enormous appetite by tearing into prey with ferocious force.

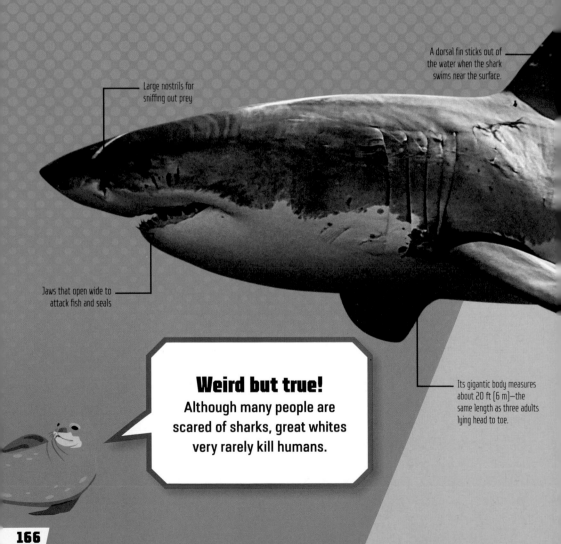

A dorsal fin sticks out of the water when the shark swims near the surface.

Large nostrils for sniffing out prey

Jaws that open wide to attack fish and seals

Its gigantic body measures about 20 ft (6 m)—the same length as three adults lying head to toe.

Weird but true!

Although many people are scared of sharks, great whites very rarely kill humans.

Super stats

Scientific name: Carcharodon carcharias
Lifespan: Up to 70 years
Length: 13-16 ft (4-5 m)
Weight: More than 1,500-2,400 lb (700-1,100 kg)
Diet: Marine mammals, fish, sharks, and sea turtles
Habitat: Mostly in temperate, coastal ocean waters
Location: Coasts of the northeastern and western United States, Chile, northern Japan, southern Australia, New Zealand, southern Africa, and the Mediterranean

Streamlined shape for strong swimming

Sharp scales cover the enormous body.

Tail powers the shark through the water

Each one of around 300 sharp teeth can be replaced if it falls out—even if that happens more than once!

Longhorn cowfish

This unusual little fish takes its name from the long horns attached to its head, which look like the horns of a cow or bull. They are there to put off predators that don't want a difficult, pointed meal! When threatened, the cowfish can also produce a deadly poison from its skin to deter attackers.

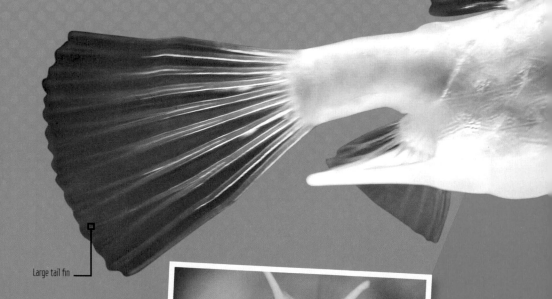

Large tail fin

Box-shaped body

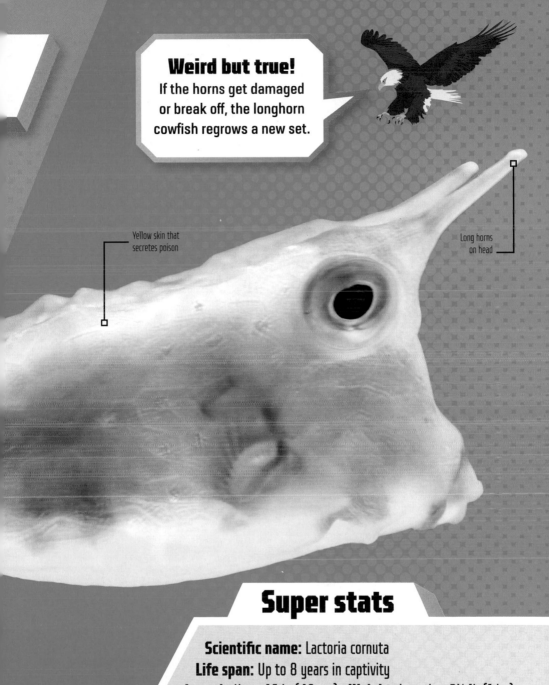

Weird but true!
If the horns get damaged or break off, the longhorn cowfish regrows a new set.

Yellow skin that secretes poison

Long horns on head

Super stats

Scientific name: Lactoria cornuta
Life span: Up to 8 years in captivity
Length: Up to 16 in (40 cm)   **Weight:** Less than 2¼ lb (1 kg)
Diet: Algae, worms, mollusks, and small crustaceans and fishes
Habitat: Coral reefs, reef flats, and protected seaward reefs
Location: Pacific and Indian Oceans and Red Sea

Birds

At least 50 billion birds soar through the skies surrounding our planet. They evolved over millions of years and are known to be related to the dinosaurs that once roamed Earth. Because most birds can fly, they have traveled the world and set up home in deserts, mountains, oceans, forests, tundra, and grasslands. The breathtaking variety of birds can be seen in their remarkable range of shapes, sizes, patterns, and colors. Now it's time to meet our feathered friends—how many do you recognize?

What is a bird?

There are about 10,000 different types of birds. They all have feathers, a pair of wings, two legs, and a beak. Most birds can fly, whether by fast flapping or gentle gliding. The ones that can't fly are fast runners or skilled swimmers.

Feathers

Wings

Beak

Lightweight body

Clawed feet

Feathers

Birds are covered in feathers made of keratin—which is also found in your hair and fingernails! They have three types of feathers. Soft, fluffy feathers cover the body for warmth; short, strong feathers keep rain off the skin; and long flight feathers on the wings and tail are used to take off, fly, and land.

Beaks

Different types of beaks help birds eat. Hunting birds, such as eagles, have hooked beaks to rip apart prey. Fishing birds have long beaks to catch slippery fish from water, while insect-eating birds have narrow, sharp beaks to carefully grab tiny prey.

Male and female

Many male birds are more brightly colored than females. This display helps the males find mates. Male ducks are multicolored compared to the duller brown females, while male peacocks spread out their tails to reveal their dazzling feathers.

Eggs

All female birds lay eggs, which have strong shells to protect the young growing inside. Most birds build nests of sticks, leaves, or mud. This provides a safe place for females to lay their eggs. The parents sit on the eggs in the nest to keep them warm and protected against predators.

Winged wonders

Birds that fly have special features to help them take off from the ground and stay airborne. Hollow bones help make them lightweight, streamlined shapes allow then to slip through the air, and they have a set of wings that they flap to keep themselves above the ground.

Wandering albatross

The wingspan of the wandering albatross is the largest of any bird, and can reach up to 11 ft (3⅖ m)—wider than a bus! The albatross uses its wings to glide for hours without flapping, and to travel up to 10,000 miles (16,000 km) in one epic journey. Its keen eyes can spot food in the form of fish, squid, or octopus in the waters below.

Enormous outstretched wings

Pairs of wandering albatrosses mate for life.

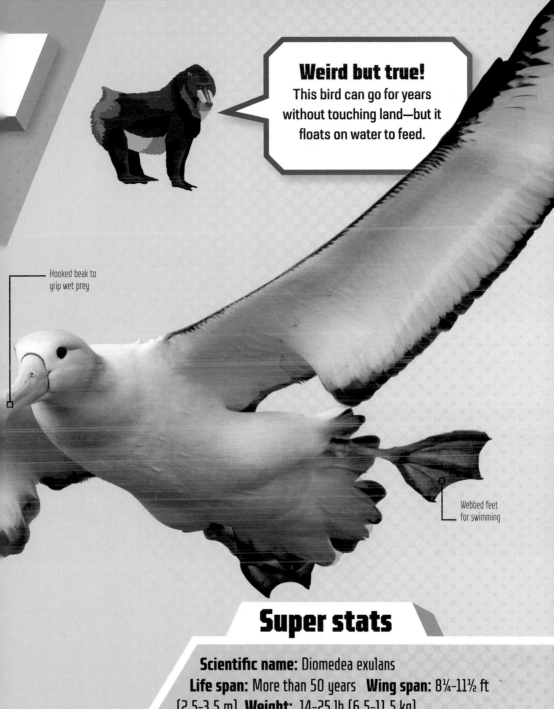

Weird but true!
This bird can go for years without touching land—but it floats on water to feed.

Hooked beak to grip wet prey

Webbed feet for swimming

Super stats

Scientific name: Diomedea exulans
Life span: More than 50 years   **Wing span:** 8¼–11½ ft (2.5–3.5 m)   **Weight:** 14–25 lb (6.5–11.5 kg)
Diet: Small marine animals
Habitat: Open ocean or sea
Location: Antarctic Ocean

Arctic tern

The Arctic tern is the migration champion, traveling all the way to the other side of the world—and back again! Every year this bird flies from the Arctic to Antarctica, before returning. As a result, the Arctic tern spends most of its time in flight.

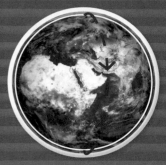

Lightweight body glides on the wind

Beak dips into water to feed on fish

Large wings for long-distance flight

Arctic terns get to enjoy two summers a year, as they fly from one summer to another.

Arctic tern: Far flyer

Head-to-head!

Some creatures make round-the-world trips every year, whether it's to breed, feed, or find warmer weather. They take to the skies, swim the seas, or trek over ground. But which of the travelers on these pages goes the farthest?

Wildebeest

Every year about 1.5 million of these great, hairy antelopes travel together through Tanzania and Kenya to follow the seasonal rains and find the best, lush grass. Joining them on their travels are other savanna creatures, such as zebra and gazelle.

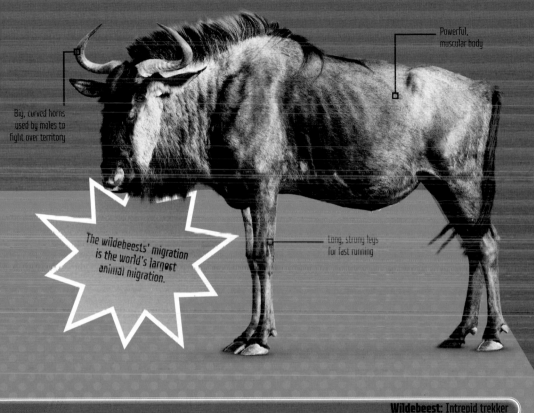

Powerful, muscular body

Big, curved horns used by males to fight over territory

The wildebeests' migration is the world's largest animal migration.

Long, strong legs for fast running

Wildebeest: Intrepid trekker

Who would win?

The Arctic tern migrates farther than any other animal. In total, it flies an astonishing 44,000 miles (71,000 km) to get to its destination. The wildebeest travels much farther than most land animals, but it still only covers 300 miles (480 km) with its big yearly trip.

Winner!

California condor

Meet the biggest bird in North America. The California condor is a type of vulture that scavenges for food on the ground. It takes flight on huge wings and can soar to impressive heights.

Weird but true!
Some California condors have wingspans of 10 ft (3 m)!

Giant black wings

Bald head

Long feathers

Super stats

Scientific name: Gymnogyps californianus
Life span: Up to 60 years   **Wingspan:** 8¼-9¾ ft (2.5-3 m)
Height: 4-4¼ ft (1.2-1.3 m)   **Weight:** 18-31 lb (8-14 kg)
Diet: Dead mammals, such as cattle and deer
Habitat: Rocky cliffs
Location: Western USA

Brown pelican

Pelicans have extraordinarily big beaks that they use like fishing nets. The birds dip their beaks underwater to catch lots of fish. A stretchy pouch inside their mouths stores the fish ready to eat.

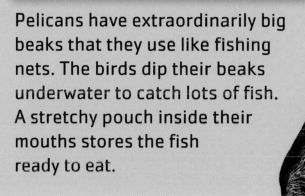

Waterproof feathers

Enormous beak for catching fish

Weird but true!

The brown pelican has room for three times more fish inside its mouth than its stomach.

Webbed feet for swimming

Super stats

Scientific name: Pelecanus occidentalis
Life span: Up to 30 years **Wingspan:** 6¾–7½ ft (2–2³⁄₁₀ m)
Height: ⁹⁄₁₀–1½ m (3–5 ft) **Weight:** About 7–8¼ lb (3¹⁄₅–3⁷⁄₁₀ kg)
Diet: Fish, such as herring **Habitat:** Coastal and marine habitats
Location: North and South America, along the Pacific, Atlantic, and Caribbean coasts

Atlantic puffin

Atlantic puffins can swim as well as soar. Their wings flap like fins to power through the water at high speed, while big webbed feet steer them in the right direction.

Waterproof feathers

Brightly colored beak

Weird but true!
The puffin's beak and tongue contain spikes to hold lots of slippery fish at once.

Wings act as fins

Webbed feet paddle through water

Super stats

Scientific name: Fratercula arctica **Life span:** 10-20 years
Wingspan: 19-25 in (47-63 cm) **Length:** About 10 in (26 cm)
Weight: About 16 oz (450 g) **Diet:** Sand eels, capelins, and herrings
Habitat: Sea cliffs in summer, open ocean and seas outside the breeding season **Location:** Arctic and North Atlantic Oceans, and their rocky coasts and islands

Snowy owl

The largest hunting bird in the Arctic region is the snowy owl. It has white feathers that provide camouflage by blending in with the snow and ice. It has excellent hearing to detect small prey moving under the snow, which it swoops down to kill.

Super stats

Scientific name: Bubo scandiaca
Life span: Up to 10 years
Length: About 26 in (65 cm)
Wingspan: 4¾–5¼ ft (147–159 cm)
Weight: 3½–6½ lb (1.5–2.9 kg)
Diet: Lemmings, rabbits, hares, voles, ducks, and geese
Habitat: Frozen, treeless tundra
Location: In and around the Arctic, and farther south during winter

Soft feathers for flying in total silence

Weird but true!
Owls cannot chew, so they swallow prey whole. Gulp!

Sharp talons to grab a tight hold of prey

Thick feathers that cover the feet for warmth

Greater flamingo

Flamingos are sociable birds that gather together in the warm waters of lakes and coastlines. A group, called a flamboyance, can include one million flamingos! They are filter feeders, using their huge bills like a sieve to take in tiny shrimps and algae, and filter out the water.

Super stats

Scientific name: Phoenicopterus roseus
Life span: 44 years
Height: 4-5 ft (1.2-15 m)
Weight: About 8¾ lb (4 kg)
Diet: Insects, shrimp, and tiny plants
Habitat: Salt pans, salty lagoons, shallow lakes, mudflats, and sandbanks **Location:** Africa, southern Asia, and Europe

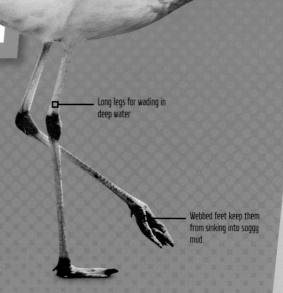

Pink feathers are the result of natural coloring in their food.

Long legs for wading in deep water

Webbed feet keep them from sinking into soggy mud.

Weird but true!
Flamingos sleep standing in the water, usually on one leg!

Secretary bird

The secretary bird rarely flies, so its long legs walk for hours at a time. It chases prey at high speed before kicking and pounding them with its powerful feet, then swallowing them whole!

Eye-catching crest of black feathers

Strong feet to kill prey

Long legs for walking great distances

Super stats

Scientific name: Sagittarius serpentarius
Life span: 10–15 years
Height: 3½–5 ft (1.1–1.5 m)
Weight: About 8¾ lb (4 kg)
Diet: Small rodents, amphibians, and reptiles
Habitat: Grassland, large cereal farms, and semi-desert with scrub
Location: Sub-Saharan Africa

Weird but true!
Secretary birds attack prey in the same way that prehistoric birds once did millions of years ago.

Andean Condor

This condor is one of the world's largest flying birds. It lives high in the snow-capped mountains of South America, where strong winds help it glide through the air. The Andean condor is a scavenger that uses its excellent vision to spot animal carcasses that it swoops down to devor.

Weird but true!
The Andean condor can fly a distance of 100 miles (160 km) without flapping its wings once.

Super stats

Scientific name: Vultur gryphus
Life span: Up to 50 years
Wingspan: Up to 10¾ ft (3 m)   **Length:** 4-4¼ ft (1.2-1.3 m)
Weight: 18-31 lb (8-14 kg)
Diet: Dead mammals, such as cattle and deer
Habitat: High mountains, lowland deserts, open grasslands, along coastlines, and in alpine regions   **Location:** Peru, Chile, Northern Venezuela, Argentina, and Colombia

Super sharp eyesight

Huge wingspan for gliding at altitude

Thick feathers for extra warmth

Males have brown eyes and females have red eyes.

Bee hummingbird

Only the size of a bee, the bee hummingbird is the world's smallest bird. At home on the Caribbean island of Cuba, this fast flier flaps its wings 80 times a second to move forward, backward, and to hover in midair. It has a long beak that is used to dip inside flowers for sweet nectar to eat.

Feathered foodies

If you want to know what a bird likes eating, look no further than its beak. The size and shape of the beak give big clues to their diet. Birds have very different beaks depending on where they live and what is available for dinner.

Meat

Eagles, hawks, and owls enjoy meat meals. These skilled hunters swoop down on prey and take hold with sharp talons before their hooked beaks tear through the meat.

Fish

Fishing birds have long beaks to stab or catch prey underwater. Herons use their beaks like swords to spear fish, while scarlet ibises pull shrimps and worms from rivers.

Nuts

Parrots are an example of a nut-eating bird. They crack open the shells with their hooked beaks.

Seeds

Birds, including sparrows and chaffinches, eat small seeds. They use their pointed beaks like parrots, to crack the seeds open.

Extraordinary eaters

The Egyptian vulture is a thief that takes the eggs of other birds and breaks them open to eat.

If food is in short supply, vampire ground finches peck at the feet of booby birds to drink the blood.

Secretary birds and snake eagles regularly eat snakes, including some of the world's most venomous species!

Nectar

Long beaks allow some birds to reach deep inside flowers for nectar. Hummingbirds are thirsty flower feeders, drinking more than their own body weight in nectar every day!

Fruit

Toucans have giant, jagged beaks to reach and grip fruit on nearby branches. Blackbirds, thrushes, and starlings also help themselves to apples and berries growing in the trees.

Insects

Birds mainly eat insects. Swallows, bluebirds, robins, and wrens all have narrow, sharp beaks to carefully target tiny bugs on the ground or in the air.

Plants

Finches like eating different parts of plants, including shoots, leaves, stems, and roots. In water, ducks have wide, flat beaks suitable for ripping apart aquatic plants.

Emu

Among the world's tallest birds, the emu reaches about the same height as an adult woman. It is too heavy to fly, so it wanders around the Australian outback, searching for small creatures, insects, plants, and fruits to eat. If it needs to run, it can reach speeds of 30 mph (50 kph).

Two sets of eyelids—to blink and to remove dust

Long, soft feathers

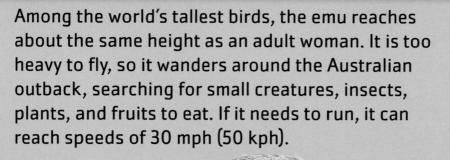

Long, strong legs for running

Weird but true!
Emus are noisy enough to be heard
1 mile (2 km) away.

Super stats

Scientific name: Dromaius novaehollandiae
Life span: 10-20 years
Height: 4½-5½ ft (1.4-1.7 m)   **Weight:** 40-106 lb (18-48 kg)
Diet: Plants and insects
Habitat: Dry, open country
Location: Australia

King penguin

At home in icy Antarctica, the king penguin keeps warm thanks to dense, waterproof feathers covering a thick layer of fat. Although it cannot fly, it is a skilled swimmer.

Weird but true!
Both penguin parents take turns heating the baby egg by placing it on their feet under their toasty tummies.

Short, strong wings for swimming

Black backs to camouflage it in water

Heavyweight body keeps the penguin underwater

Super stats

Scientific name: Aptenodytes patagonicus
Life span: About 26 years
Height: 33-37 in (85-95 cm)   **Weight:** Up to 45 lb (20 kg)
Diet: Fish, especially lantern fish
Habitat: Shores and valleys
Location: Sub-Antarctic islands

Mute swan

The mute swan starts its life as a gray, downy chick, called a cygnet. As it grows, its gray down are replaced by white feathers. It can walk on land, fly in the air, and swim on ponds and lakes. Most animals will have more than one mate, but this bird stays together with its mate for life.

Graceful neck dips underwater to feed

Raised wings to glide across water

Weird but true!
Some mute swan wingspans stretch to more than 6.5 ft (2 m)!

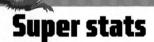

Webbed feet for swimming

Super stats

Scientific name: Cygnus olor
Life span: Up to 21 years
Height: 4½-5¼ ft (1.4-1.6 m)   **Weight:** Around 50 lb (23 kg)
Diet: Underwater plants
Habitat: Rivers, ponds, and lakes
Location: Europe and the Atlantic Coast of the USA

Blakiston's fish owl

Meet the world's biggest owl! The Blakiston's fish owl nests in enormous tree holes in remote forests. It rarely flies—instead, it stays on the ground by rivers, ready to catch fish.

Super stats

Scientific name: Bubo blakistoni
Life span: More than 20 years
Height: 24-28 in (60-72 cm)
Weight: 6½-7 ⅞ lb (2.9-3.6 kg)
Diet: Fish, lizards, frogs, and water rats.
Habitat: Dense forest near waterways and wooded coastlines
Location: China, Japan, and northeastern Asia

Thick feathers to keep warm

Bright eyes for sharp sight

Weird but true!
The Blakiston's fish owl can catch fish that are twice its own body weight.

Heavyweight body suits life on the ground

Mandarin duck

The male mandarin duck is instantly recognised by its multicoloured feathers. This brilliant display attracts females, who are much duller in colour. The mandarin duck feeds on seeds and bugs up in the trees or down on the water. It can also take to the skies to fly long distances.

Super stats

Scientific name: Aix galericulata
Life span: Around 6 years
Height: 16-19½ in (41-49 cm)
Weight: 18-22 oz (500-625 g)
Diet: Plants, seeds, nuts, and insects
Habitat: Lakes, pools, and rivers
Location: China, Japan, Korea, and parts of Russia

Striking colors of the male

Females have mostly brown feathers.

Weird but true!
Unlike most ducks, the mandarin duck nests in trees rather than on water.

Big eyes to see in the dark

Sharp claws to grip branches

Common toucan

This big bird lives in the rain forests of South America. It spends most of its time in the branches of trees, looking for juicy fruits to eat. Its large beak is used to pick ripe fruits, and is also handy for scaring off predators.

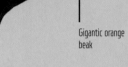

Gigantic orange beak

Weird but true!
The big beak is very lightweight because it is hollow inside.

Shiny black feathers

Super stats

Scientific name: Ramphastos toco
Life span: Up to 20 years
Length: 21½–24 in (55–61 cm)
Weight: 18–30 oz (500–850 g)
Diet: Fruit and small animals
Habitat: Rain forests **Location:** South America

Common kingfisher

The fast-flying kingfisher appears as a streak of brilliant blue by rivers or streams. It perches on branches to spot fish moving in the waters below, then dives into the water headfirst to grab the fish with its beak.

Bright blue feathers

Short wings for fast flight

Orange belly

Dagger-shaped beak

Weird but true!
The kingfisher's beak shape inspired the design of the super-fast Japanese bullet train!

Super stats

Scientific name: Alcedo atthis
Life span: 7-21 years
Height: Around 6½ in (16 cm)   **Weight:** 1-1¼ oz (25-35 g)
Diet: Fish and small crustaceans, such as prawns and crabs
Habitat: Near streams, canals, ponds, and small rivers and lakes
Location: Europe, Asia, and Africa

Golden eagle

Named after the gold on its head, the golden eagle ranks among the most powerful birds of prey. It soars through the air on the hunt for targets on the ground, then dives down at high speed to grab prey with its razor-sharp talons.

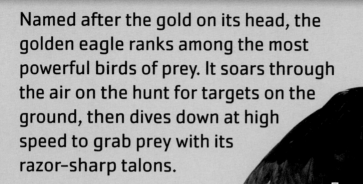

Incredible eyesight

Huge wingspan

Sharp talons

Weird but true!
This is one of the only birds that can kill with its feet.

Super stats

Scientific name: Aquila chrysaetos
Lifespan: About 23 years
Length: About 3 ft (90 cm)   **Weight:** 8–11⅔ lb (3.5–5.3 kg)
Diet: Carrion, small mammals, birds, fish, and insects
Habitat: Open moorlands, hills, and grasslands
Location: North America, Mexico, Asia, northern Africa, and Europe

White-bellied sea eagle

This eagle is built for catching fish, with rough skin beneath its talons that help it grasp slippery prey. It lives and hunts near the rivers, lakes, and seas of southeast Asia and Australia. Fish make up half its diet, and the rest is sea snakes, birds, rodents, and carrion.

Super stats

Scientific name: Haliaeetus leucogaster
Life span: Around 30 years
Length: 28-36 in (70-90 cm)
Weight: 4 5/8-7½ lb (2.1-3.4 kg)
Diet: Fish, turtles, and sea snakes, and occasionally birds and mammals
Habitat: Coastal waters, islands, rivers, and lakes
Location: Australia, New Guinea, Southeast Asia, and the southwest Pacific

Big, hooked beak

Bright white tummy

Weird but true!
White-bellied sea eagles reuse their nests each year, unlike most birds.

Long, dark talons

199

Common swift

There is no stopping the common swift. Not only is it one of the fastest birds in level (nondiving) flight, but every year the swift migrates almost 6,000 miles (10,000 km) from Europe to Africa. This means it spends 10 months of the year in flight!

The common swift can sleep in the air!

Forked tail

Long, narrow wings

Common swift: Feathered racer

Head-to-head!

It's not just birds that have mastered the art of speedy flying—the bat is a strong condender for quickest animal in the sky. So which one would win in a race between the fastest bird and bat?

Mexican free-tail bat

Bats are the only mammals that can fly. Far and away the fastest bat is the Mexican free-tail bat. A streamlined body shape, short fur, and long flight wings help it achieve its record-breaking speeds.

Mexican free-tail bats can fly 100 miles (160 km) a night on the hunt for moths and insects.

Pointed ears

Long, narrow wings

Large tail

Mexican free-tail bat: Quick as a flash

Who would win?

The fastest common swift flight ever measured was clocked at 70 mph (112 km/h). But the Mexican free-tail bat can reach speeds of an astonishing 100 mph (160 km/h)! That means the mammal wins.

Winner!

Kookaburra

Known as the "laughing kookaburra," this bird's noisy call sounds just like loud laughter. It can be heard at dawn and dusk in the forests of Australia, where it hunts insects, snakes, and rodents. It is part of the kingfisher family, but it has much duller feathers than most species.

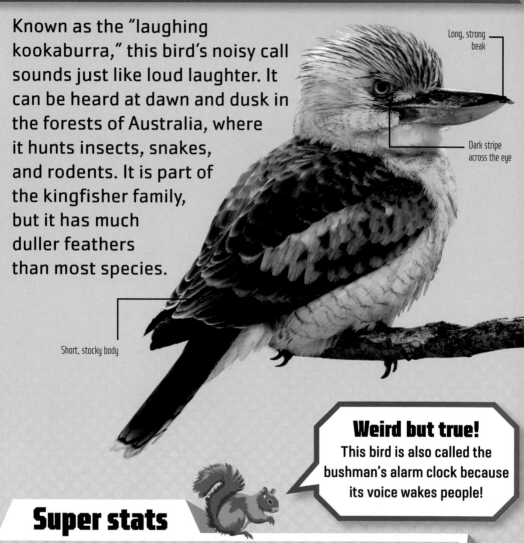

Long, strong beak

Dark stripe across the eye

Short, stocky body

Weird but true!

This bird is also called the bushman's alarm clock because its voice wakes people!

Super stats

Scientific name: Dacelo novaeguineae
Life span: Up to 20 years
Length: Around 15.5 in (40 cm)   **Weight:** 11–12 oz (325–350 g)
Diet: Insects, snakes, and small birds
Habitat: Eucalyptus forest and woodland
Location: East and southwest Australia

Magnificent frigatebird

The male magnificent frigatebird has a unique way of attracting mates. It calls out while blowing up a pouch on its throat, like a big red balloon. This American seabird spend its time flying over water on the lookout for fish. As its feathers are not waterproof, frigate birds dip only their beaks in the water, to catch fish but keep dry.

Lightweight body for flying

Hooked beak

Inflated throat pouch

Super stats

Scientific name:
Fregata magnificens
Life span: 15–25 years
Length: Around 3¼ ft (100 cm)
Weight: 2½–3¾ lb (1.1–1.7 kg)
Diet: Fish
Habitat: Coastal mangrove swamps
Location: Atlantic and Pacific Oceans and inshore waters

Weird but true!
Frigatebirds often steal fish from other birds in flight!

Scissor-tailed flycatcher

This bird is named after its unusual tail—which looks like a pair of open scissors. The scissor-tailed flycatcher chases bugs flying through the air, while using its flexible tail to change direction at high speed. Every year, the flycatcher migrates from the USA to Central America for warmer weather.

Long beak for hunting

Large wings for flying

Long-tailed widowbird

Dramatic tail feathers give this African bird its name. Males use the long tails to attract females. The widowbird has a lovely warbling voice and forages in grasslands looking for seeds and bugs to eat.

Sharp beak to grab prey

Super stats

Scientific name: Tyrannus forficatus
Life span: 10-15 years
Length: 7½-15 in (19-38 cm)
Weight: Around 1 ⅜ oz (40 g)
Diet: Insects, such as grasshoppers, beetles, and bees
Habitat: Grassland and savanna
Location: North and Central America

Weird but true!
Pairs of male and female flycatchers perform dances in the sky with twists, turns, and somersaults.

Forked tail

Super stats

Scientific name: Euplectes progne
Life span: Unknown
Length: Around 23⅝ in (60 cm)
Weight: Unknown
Diet: Mainly grass seeds and occasionally insects
Habitat: Grassland
Location: Central and south Africa

Weird but true!
The widowbird's tail feathers can measure twice as long as the rest of its body.

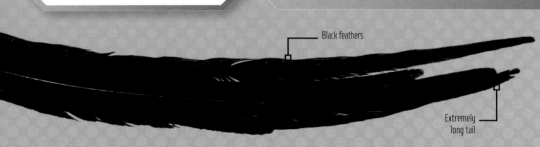

Black feathers

Extremely long tail

Great blue heron

Say hello to North America's biggest heron. The great blue heron wades along rivers, marshes, and coastlines on the lookout for prey. The flexible neck and sharp beak are used to attack fish underwater. But this heron is also a strong flier that can dive for rodents and insects on the ground.

Lightweight body

Huge beak for catching fish

Super stats

Scientific name: Ardea herodias
Life span: Around 15 years
Length: 3¼-4½ ft (97-137 cm)
Weight: 4½-7¼ lb (2-3.25 kg)
Diet: Fish, frogs, small mammals, birds, and insects
Habitat: Fresh and salt water, swamps, and dry land
Location: North America

Long legs for wading

Weird but true!
The great blue heron looks blue when its flight feathers spread out in the air.

Shoebill

This tall African bird is a terrifying hunter in swamps and wetlands. It stands still like a statue until it spots a lungfish, eel, frog, or snake moving in the water. Then the shoebill strikes! It throws itself underwater open-mouthed and the prey is caught in the gaping beak.

Head crest

Chunky shoe shaped abeak

Gray feathers

Weird but true!

The shoebill is also called the whale-headed stork because its huge beak is the shape of a whale.

Super stats

Scientific name: Balaeniceps rex
Life span: Around 35 years
Length: Around 4 ft (1.2 m)
Weight: 12–14 lb (5.5–6.5 kg)
Diet: Lungfish, small turtles, crocodiles, and mammals
Habitat: Swamps
Location: Central East Africa

Master weavers

Weaverbirds create some of the most intricate structures in nature. The males weave sticks, leaves, roots, and grass to make nests hanging from trees in Africa. These constructions attract passing female weaverbirds. When the female lays her eggs, they are kept safe inside from predators. Sometimes, one gigantic nest can house entire communities of weaverbirds!

Blue tit

Black stripes across the eyes

Bright blue feathers

Small, lightweight body for flight

This little bird is easy to spot with its bright blue wings and yellow belly. It lives in European woodlands and forests, but is also a regular visitor to parks and gardens where there are plenty of insects and seeds. Blue tits are friendly and sociable, and often fly in large flocks.

Weird but true!
Blue tits are tiny gymnasts that can hang upside down from trees in order to reach food.

Super stats

Scientific name: Cyanistes caeruleus
Life span: Around 3 years
Length: 4¾ in (12 cm)   **Weight:** ⅜ oz (11 g)
Diet: Insects and spiders
Habitat: Woodland, hedgerows, parks, and gardens
Location: Europe, north Africa and west Asia

Blue-throated hummingbird

This small bird is always on the go. It can be found flitting around the mountain ranges of the USA and Mexico, with its tiny wings beating super fast. It stops to feed on the sweet nectar inside flowers, sometimes visiting 2,000 flowers a day!

Lightweight body

Long beak to reach inside flowers

Shiny blue feathers at the throat

Weird but true!
Hummingbirds use up energy so quickly they must eat their own body weight in nectar every day to survive.

Super stats

Scientific name: Lampornis clemenciae
Life span: Up to 12 years
Length: Around 5 in (13 cm) **Weight:** ¼ oz (6–9 g)
Diet: Mostly nectar, and occasionally small insects and spiders
Habitat: Wooded streams in canyons
Location: Southwest USA and Mexico

Common raven

This big black bird ranks among the largest crows. The raven hunts rats and mice but also feeds on insects, seeds, and even poo. Male ravens perform acrobatic displays to attract females. They then make massive nests with their mates.

Large, thick beak

Scarlet macaw

Macaws are the world's biggest parrots. The scarlet macaw lives in the tropical rain forests of South America and is named after its vivid red feathers. This eye-catching, energetic parrot uses its great beak to pick fruit and break open nuts and seeds.

Weird but true!
The world's oldest scarlet macaw, named Charlie, was 114 years old.

Long wings

Glossy black feathers

Weird but true!
Some ravens nest on Mount Everest, the world's tallest mountain.

Super stats

Scientific name: Corvus corax
Life span: About 13 years   **Length:** About 26 in (66 cm)
Weight: 2¼–3¼ lb (1–1.5 kg)
Diet: Carrion, small crustaceans, fish, rodents, fruit, grain, eggs, and garbage
Habitat: Boreal and mountain forests, coastal cliffs, tundra, and desert   **Location:** Western and northern North America

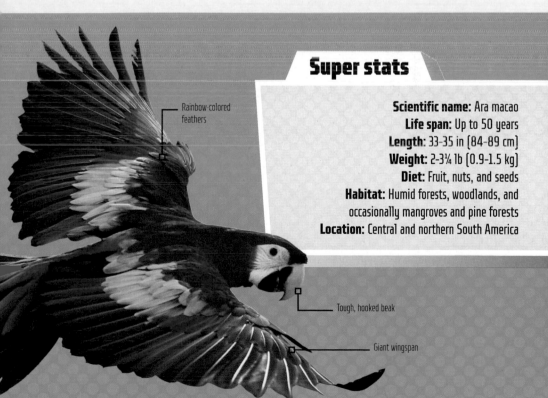

Rainbow-colored feathers

Super stats

Scientific name: Ara macao
Life span: Up to 50 years
Length: 33–35 in (84–89 cm)
Weight: 2–3¼ lb (0.9–1.5 kg)
Diet: Fruit, nuts, and seeds
Habitat: Humid forests, woodlands, and occasionally mangroves and pine forests
Location: Central and northern South America

Tough, hooked beak

Giant wingspan

Eagle

Like most birds of prey, eagles have sharper vision than any other creature. They can see very long distances and adjust their eyes to zoom in and focus on an object in amazing detail. They can also see more shades of color than we can see.

Eagles can see at least five times farther than people can.

Huge wingspan

Sharp vision

Strong talons

Powerful beak

Eagle: Eyes of a champion

Head-to-head!

Incredible eyesight makes all the difference in the animal kingdom. It can help with hunting prey, escaping predators, and traveling long distances. But which of these two excellent–eyed creatures has the better vision?

Mantis shrimp

This small shrimp has an unusually large amount of color receptors—the parts of the eye that allow us to see color. It can see types of light that are invisible to any other animal. Scientists think this might be to see types of light reflected off each other's bodies, which act like messages to communicate.

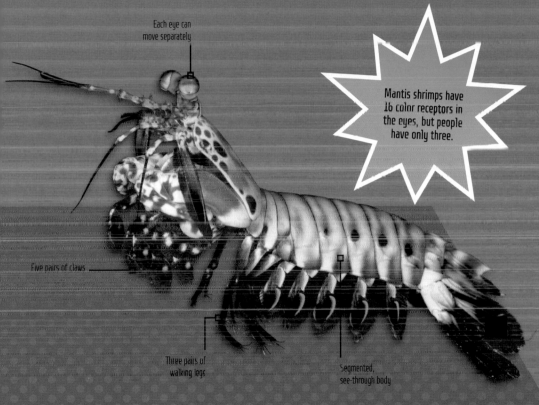

Each eye can move separately

Mantis shrimps have 16 color receptors in the eyes, but people have only three.

Five pairs of claws

Three pairs of walking legs

Segmented, see-through body

Mantis shrimp: Rainbow vision

Who would win?

These animals' eyes are impressive in different ways. The eagle can see farther, but the mantis shrimp can see types of light that no other animal is known to be able to see—which means you decide!

You decide!

Indian peafowl

The male peafowl is called a peacock —and he puts on a dazzling display to attract a mate. If a female comes near, he raises his shiny blue and green feathers and spreads them out to form a fantastic fan. The female peafowl, the peahen, looks very different. She has darker and duller feathers.

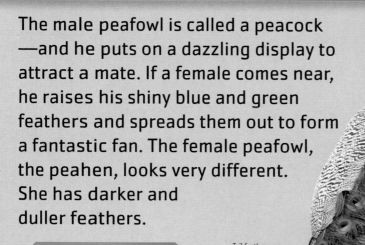

Dramatic head crest

Beautiful eyespots

Tail feathers that spread out

Weird but true!
A peacock's tail can contain 200 feathers.

Super stats

Scientific name: Pavo crisatus
Life span: 15-20 years
Length: 70-98 in (180-250 cm)   **Weight:** 8-13 lb (3.8-6 kg)
Diet: Grain, insects, small reptiles and mammals, berries, figs, leaves, seeds, and flower parts
Habitat: Tall, open trees   **Location:** Southeast Asia

Bald eagle

From amazing eyesight to sharp talons, this powerful predator is perfectly equipped for airborne hunting in North America. The bald eagle hunts fish, rodents, and even young deer. It is also brave enough to steal prey from the claws of other birds!

White feathers, making the head look bald

Sharp eyes

Strong talons for grabbing prey

Weird but true!

This eagle builds one of the biggest nests of any bird—weighing up to two tons!

Super stats

Scientific name: Haliaeetus leucocephalus
Life span: Up to 28 years
Length: About 28-40 in (71-102 cm)   **Weight:** 6½-14 lb (2.9-6.3 kg)
Diet: Mainly carrion and fish, and occasionally fish stolen from ospreys
Habitat: Woods, near water
Location: North America

Ostrich

The ostrich has a big, bulky body and can weigh as much as two adult men—making it the world's biggest bird. Although it is too heavy to fly, it can run faster than any other bird. Ostriches race through the African bushland at high speed and even sleep standing up, so they can run at the first sign of danger.

Small head

Sharp eyes

Long neck

Thick feathers

Long legs

Weird but true!
The ostrich can reach speeds of 45 mph (75 km/h) and outrun a racehorse!

Super stats

Scientific name: Struthio camelus
Life span: 30-40 years   **Height:** 7-9 ft (2-2.7 m)
Weight: 220-350 lb (100-158 kg)
Diet: Vegetation and insects
Habitat: Savannah and desert   **Location:** Africa

Southern cassowary

Head horn

As well as being a very tall bird, the southern cassowary also stands out for its bright blue head, topped by a horn. Because it cannot fly, it walks through the tropical forests of Australia and New Guinea on the lookout for fallen fruit to eat. If a predator dares to come close, the cassowary fights back with its oversized claws.

Weird but true!

The cassowary's head horn is made of keratin, the same substance in your hair and fingernails.

Super stats

Scientific name: Casuarius casuarius
Life span: Up to 40 years
Height: 60-72 in (1.5-1.8 m)
Weight: 6 ⅝-12¾ lb (3-5.8 kg)
Diet: Fruit, snails, and fungi
Habitat: Rain forest
Location: North Queensland, Australia

Long legs

Long, sharp claws

Red Kite

As the name suggests, red kites are fantastic fliers that soar the skies of Europe and northern Africa on the lookout for carcasses on the ground. They mainly scavenge roadkill and leftover prey, but they will also hunt baby birds and small rodents.

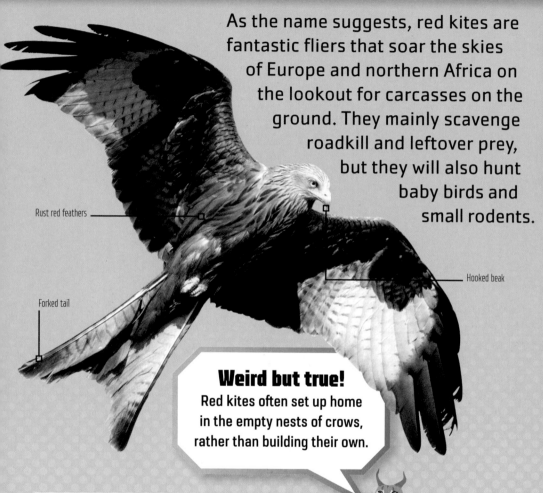

Rust red feathers

Hooked beak

Forked tail

Weird but true!
Red kites often set up home in the empty nests of crows, rather than building their own.

Super stats

Scientific name: Milvus milvus
Life span: Up to 25 years
Length: 23½–26 in (60-65 cm)   **Weight:** 34-43 oz (950-1,200 g)
Diet: Mostly dead animals, and some birds and small mammals
Habitat: Open woodland and farmland
Location: Europe and northwestern Africa

Lappet-faced vulture

This African bird uses its super size and strength to win its prey. Other vultures back off from animal carcasses and let the lappet-faced vulture enjoy the feast. However, this vulture will also hunt small creatures and eat tiny termites as they leave their nests.

Super stats

Scientific name: Torgos tracheliotus
Life span: 20–50 years
Length: Up to 41 in (105 cm)
Weight: 31 lb (14 kg)
Diet: Dead animals and small reptiles, fish, birds, and mammals
Habitat: Open areas and semidesert
Location: Sub-Saharan Africa, Saudi Arabia, Yemen, and Oman

Giant wings

Featherless head

Big, strong beak

Weird but true!
Vultures are clean birds that bathe in water after messy meals.

221

Birds and dinosaurs

The closest living relatives to dinosaurs are birds! Our feathered friends' ancestors ruled planet Earth about 200 million years ago. And there are plenty of similarities between the two animals...

Hollow bones

Some dinosaurs had hollow bones for flight. Birds today have such hollow bones that their skeletons weigh less than their feathers.

Dinosaurs had three-clawed hands, like the three digits of birds.

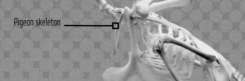

Pigeon skeleton

Pygostyle

Clawed feet

Many dinosaurs had similar clawed feet to bird feet. They used them to grab prey, too.

Bony tail

Dinosaurs had a small bony tail. This is like the tail of birds, called the pygostyle.

Feathers

Some dinosaurs were covered in feathers. Birds are the only creatures with feathers today.

Early bird

Meet Archaeopteryx, meaning "ancient wing." This is the best example of a birdlike creature from the dinosaur era. Not only did it have the head, teeth, claws, and tail of a dinosaur but it also shared the same thick feathers and big wings, which allowed it to fly a short distance.

The arm bones of dinosaurs gradually evolved into birdlike wings.

Descended from dinosaurs

Hoatzin

This small South American bird has claws on each wing. Some dinosaurs had this feature too.

Chicken

The world's most common bird shares plenty with dinosaurs. It has similar clawed feet, protective feathers, a toothless beak, and wings rarely used for flight.

Bird behavior

Dinosaurs and birds are not only linked by the way they look. They both build nests and lay eggs. When the eggs hatch, the young are cared for by their parents.

 # Crow

Found in most parts of the world, crows are entirely black birds with big brains. Their amazing ability to use tools in nature and communicate with each other make them one of the world's cleverest birds.

A large beak produces a loud call.

Super stats

Scientific name: Corvus
Life span: About 13 years
Length: 20 in (50 cm)
Weight: 19–21 oz (540–600 g)
Diet: Berries, insects, the eggs of other birds, and carrion
Habitat: Open areas with nearby trees, farmland, and grassland
Location: Worldwide, except southern South America

Weird but true!
Studies have shown that crows recognize and remember human faces.

Shiny black feathers

Starling

This bird seems black from a distance, but if you look closely you will spot different colored feathers. The starling spends all its time in a huge flock, flying during the day and sleeping close together at night.

Bright yellow beak

Glossy green and purple feathers

Strong feet

Weird but true!
A murmuration is a flock of hundreds or thousands of starlings that swoop and soar in the evenings.

Super stats

Scientific name: Sturnus vulgaris
Life span: 1-5 years
Length: About 8½ in (21 cm)   **Weight:** 2-3¼ oz (60-96 g)
Diet: Insects, earthworms, seeds, and fruit
Habitat: Parks, gardens, and farmland
Location: Worldwide, except polar regions

Owlet nightjar

This little bird lives in Australia and the surrounding islands, and usually sets up home with a partner. During the day, the pair hide in hollow trees to avoid being seen. By night, they fly through the woodlands, hunting for insects in the air or on the ground.

Large eyes

Whiskery face

Long claws

Weird but true!
The tiny owlet nightjar has been known to catch snakes.

Super stats

Scientific name: Aegotheles cristatus
Life span: Unknown
Length: 8½-10 in (21-25 cm)   **Weight:** 1 ⅝ oz (45 g)
Diet: Beetles, caterpillars, spiders, and millipedes
Habitat: Open woodland, mallee and other scrub, and waterside trees
Location: Australia

Tawny frogmouth

This bird gets its name from its wide, froglike beak, which gapes open to catch insects. The tawny frogmouth hunts at night, camouflaging itself in the trees before swooping down on unsuspecting frogs, birds, snails, and slugs.

Super stats

Scientific name: Podargus strigoides
Life span: Up to 10 years
Length: 13½–21 in (34-53 cm)
Weight: Up to 24 oz (680 g)
Diet: Mainly insects, occasionally snails, frogs, lizards, and small birds
Habitat: Forests and woods
Location: Australia, Tasmania, and New Guinea

Big, bright eyes

Bristly beak to detect flying insect prey

Weird but true!
The tawny frogmouth is sometimes mistaken for the dead branch of a tree.

Soft feathers for silent flight

Victoria crowned pigeon

This colorful bird is one of the largest types of pigeons. The Victoria crowned pigeon only takes flight to escape danger. Down on the ground, it spends its time foraging on the forest floor for fruit, seeds, grains, insects, and worms. It is a sociable animal and often forages for food in groups.

Sharp, hooked beak

Red eyes

Dramatic head crest

Super stats

Scientific name: Goura victoria
Life span: 20-25 years
Length: 26-29 in (66-74 cm)
Weight: About 5½ lb (2.5 kg)
Diet: Fruits, seeds, and insects
Habitat: Swamp, sago palm, and dry forests
Location: Indonesia and Papua New Guinea

Big, heavy body

Beautiful feathers

Weird but true!
This bird is named after the UK's Queen Victoria.

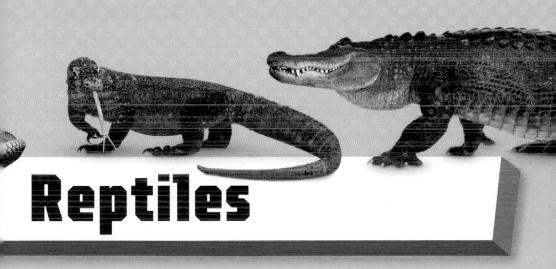

Reptiles

Reptiles once ruled the Earth in the form of dinosaurs—and some of their descendents are still around today. In this chapter you'll meet species such as these, as well as some of the most venomous creatures in the world. The cold-blooded reptile family includes deadly predators, such as the Komodo dragon; gentle herbivores, such as the green sea turtle; and some animals, such as the flying gecko, that have developed extraordinary ways to survive.

What is a reptile?

Reptiles are a group of cold-blooded animals that includes lizards, snakes, crocodiles, tortoises, and turtles. Dinosaurs were reptiles, too. Like mammals (that's you!), reptiles are vertebrates and they use their lungs to breathe.

What kind of babies do reptiles have?

Most reptiles lay eggs in nests on land. Days, weeks, or months later their babies hatch. Reptile babies look like smaller versions of the adults, and most reptile species do not care for their young.

Some reptiles give birth to live young. These include pythons, boas, and some lizards.

Are reptiles slimy?

Reptiles have tough, dry skin covered with scales or bony plates (or both). Lizards shed the outer layer of their skin in chunks, while snakes shed it in one piece. This allows them to grow bigger or to replace worn-out scales.

Many reptiles become inactive (they don't move) in winter to stay warm.

How do reptiles keep warm?

Unlike warm-blooded mammals, reptiles don't have hair to keep them warm or sweat glands to keep them cool. They are the same temperature as their surroundings. If they're cold, they find a sunny spot for warmth.

What do reptiles eat?

Most reptiles hunt and eat other animals, such as insects, frogs, birds, mammals, and fish. However, land tortoises are herbivores, munching on leaves and grasses instead.

Yellow-bellied slider

Weird, but true!
If space is limited in a sunny area, yellow-bellied sliders will stack on top of each other to get the best spot.

These turtles like to live in swamps, marshlands, slow-moving rivers, ponds, and wetlands. They get their name from their yellow plastrons (bottom shells), but they often have yellow stripes on their necks, legs, and carapaces (upper shells), too.

Carapace

Female yellow-bellied sliders can be up to 4 in (10 cm) longer than males.

Plastron

Super stats

Scientific name: Trachemys scripta scripta
Life span: 30 years or more
Weight: ¼–½ oz (7-14 g)   **Length:** 5-8 in (12.5-20.3 cm)
Diet: Insects, fish, and tadpoles   **Habitat:** Lakes, swamps, rivers, and ponds
Location: Some southern states in the USA and parts of Central America

Green anole

Like many reptiles, green anoles like to bask in the sun all day. At night, these lizards sleep in trees and bushes. Females lay their eggs (one at a time) in leaf litter and the damp remains of plants.

Weird, but true!

Green anoles are sometimes mistakenly called chameleons, since they can change color from bright green to brown in the shade.

long, slim tail

Both males and females have large, expandable throat fans.

Large pads on the green anole's toes help it to keep its balance on vertical surfaces, such as tree trunks.

Super stats

Scientific name: Anolis carolinensis **Life span:** Up to 7 years
Weight: 1/10-1/4 oz (3-7 g) **Length:** 5-8 in (13-20 cm) **Diet:** Small insects, such as crickets, grasshoppers, flies, and butterflies
Habitat: Arboreal (trees) **Location:** Southern United States

Banded sea krait

This is a sea snake, which means it looks slightly different from land snakes. It has a flat, oar-shaped tail, which helps it to swim. It is one of the most venomous snakes in the world.

Flattened tail

Green iguana

These large lizards might look fierce, but they mostly eat plants. Their long claws make them excellent at climbing trees, and their green and gray bodies are ideal camouflage. Not all green iguanas are actually green though—some are orange!

Green skin is ideal camouflage.

Males have larger dewlaps (throat flaps) to attract females.

Long, sharp claws are great for defense as well as climbing.

Weird, but true!

Sea snakes have an extra-large lung to help them breathe underwater, and also to help them to float.

Super stats

Scientific name: Laticauda colubrina
Life span: Around 10 years in captivity
Weight: 1½-4 lb (0.6-1.8 kg)
Length: Up to 4 ft (1.3 m)
Diet: Eels and small fish
Habitat: Coral reefs and rocky shores
Location: Eastern Indian and western Pacific oceans

Striped markings warn predators to stay away.

Short fangs

Weird, but true!

Some green iguanas can weigh up to 22 lb (10 kg)—that's twice as heavy as most house cats!

Super stats

Scientific name: Iguana iguana
Life span: Around 20 years
Weight: 11 lb (5 kg)
Length: 5-6½ ft (1.5-2 m)
Diet: Leaves, buds, flowers, and fruits of fig trees
Habitat: Rain forests, near rivers
Location: Central and South America

Long, whiplike tail can be used against predators.

Long legs

Kuhl's flying gecko

Weird, but true!
This gecko often rests on a tree with its head pointed downward, ready to "take off" quickly if it needs to.

This tree-dwelling lizard has a very clever way of escaping from predators— it simply jumps and glides through the air to the next tree. It's not exactly "flying," but it works!

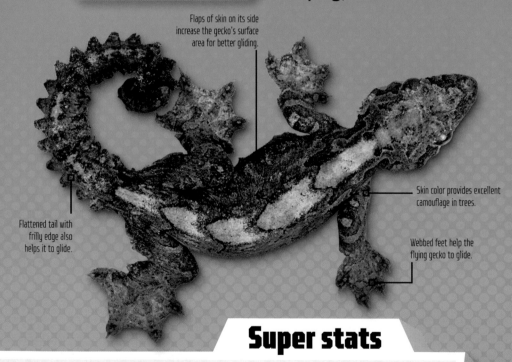

Flaps of skin on its side increase the gecko's surface area for better gliding.

Skin color provides excellent camouflage in trees.

Flattened tail with frilly edge also helps it to glide.

Webbed feet help the flying gecko to glide.

Super stats

Scientific name: Gekko (Ptychozoon) kuhli
Life span: Unknown in the wild, but up to 8 years in captivity
Weight: Unknown **Length:** 8 in (20 cm)
Diet: Insects and bugs, including crickets, roaches, and mealworms
Habitat: Rain forests
Location: Southeast Asia

Armadillo lizard

Just like its namesake mammal, the armadillo lizard curls up when threatened. It grabs its tail in its mouth to form a protective shield out of the thick, spiked scales along its head, back, and tail.

Super stats

Scientific name: Cordylus cataphractus
Life span: Unknown in the wild, up to 20 years in captivity
Length: Up to 6 in (16 cm)
Weight: 8–17 lb (3–8 kg)
Diet: Insects and spiders
Habitat: Mountains and rocky hills
Location: Southern Africa

Weird, but true!

Armadillo lizards are some of the only lizards to feed their young.

Tail in mouth to form a protective ring

This shape makes the armadillo lizard harder to attack.

Tough neck spines

Soft belly needs protecting from predators, such as birds of prey.

The scales on its back are almost square.

Green sea turtle

This turtle spends most of its life in warm, tropical oceans. When it's time to lay her eggs, the female green sea turtle digs a nest in a sandy beach. Once hatched, the baby turtles dig themselves out of the nest and rush to the safety of the sea.

Streamlined shell (carapace) to help the turtle move through the water easily

Sharp beak for tearing plants

Bottom of the shell (plastron) joins the top along the sides.

Long, paddle-shaped flippers to help push the turtle through the water

Weird but true!
Female sea turtles often return to the same spot every year to lay their eggs—many go to the beach where they were born!

Super stats

Scientific name: Chelonia mydas
Life span: 70 years or more
Length: Up to 5 ft (1.5 m)   **Weight:** About 700 lb (317.5 kg)
Diet: Seagrasses and algae   **Habitat:** Oceans
Location: Subtropical and temperate regions of the Atlantic, Pacific, and Indian Oceans, and in the Mediterranean Sea

Green basilisk

With three impressive crests, a long tail, and bright green skin, this lizard stands out from the crowd. The green basilisk's back and tail crests help it swim. Scientists think the head crest helps it attract a mate.

Super stats

Scientific name: Basiliscus plumifrons
Life span: Up to 10 years
Length: 23½–35 in (60–90 cm)
Weight: About 7 oz (198.5 g)
Diet: Insects and other small animals, flowers, and fruit
Habitat: Flooded forests
Location: Central and South America

Weird but true!
This lizard has an amazing escape trick—it can run across the surface of water on its hind legs to escape from predators!

Yellow eyes

Shorter front limbs

Long, flattened toes on hind feet help the lizard stick to the surface of the water

Long tail

Green coloring to help blend in with surroundings

Slow worm

Despite its name, this legless lizard is more likely to be confused with a snake than a worm. But there's an easy way to tell them apart—if it blinks, it's definitely a slow worm. Snakes can't blink because they don't have eyelids!

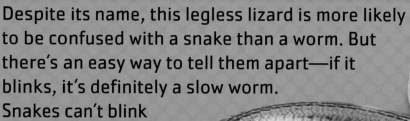

Smooth, scaly body that grows up to 20 in (50 cm) long

Tokay gecko

This large lizard gets its name from the mating call of the males, which sounds a bit like "tokay." Thanks to the pads on the ends of its fingers and toes, the tokay gecko can stick to almost any surface.

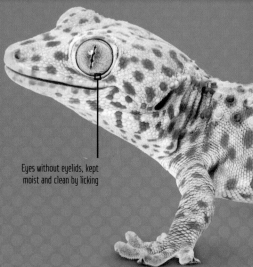

Eyes without eyelids, kept moist and clean by licking

Central stripe showing that this is a female slow worm

Super stats

Scientific name: Anguis fragilis
Life span: Up to 20 years
Length: 16-20 in (40-50 cm)
Weight: ¾-3½ oz (20-100 g)
Diet: Soft-bodied invertebrates, such as earthworms, insect larvae, spiders, and some vertebrates
Habitat: Moist grassy areas, with scrub or hedgerows
Location: Mainland Europe and the UK

Weird but true!

A slow worm can shed the end of its tail to escape a predator—then grow it back!

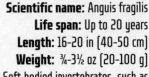

Super stats

Scientific name: Gekko gecko
Life span: About 10 years in captivity
Length: 8-14 in (20-35 cm)   **Weight:** Unknown
Diet: Invertebrates, such as moths, locusts, and grasshoppers, small rats, mice, and snakes
Habitat: Rain forests and man-made environments
Location: Southeast Asia

Weird but true!

The tokay gecko lays two soft, sticky eggs at a time, which stick to whatever they were laid on then harden over time.

Spots for camouflage

Tail can be shed if a predator grabs it.

Spectacled caiman

Also known as the common caiman, the spectacled caiman lives in freshwater habitats such as lakes and rivers. It rarely leaves the water—if there is a drought, it will burrow into mud instead.

Broad snout

Olive-green scales

Large jaws can snap up mammals the size of a pig.

Weird but true!
One of the ways that caimans attract mates is to blow bubbles! Alligators and crocodiles do this too.

Super stats

Scientific name: Caiman crocodilus
Life span: 30-40 years
Length: 8 ft (2.4 m) or more **Weight:** 15-128 lb (7-58 kg)
Diet: Fish, frogs, turtles, crabs, and snails
Habitat: Swamps and rivers
Location: Central and South America, from Mexico to Uruguay

King Cobra

The king cobra is the world's longest venomous snake. To scare off predators, it lifts up the front third of its body so that it stands 5 ft (1.5m) tall, spreads out its hood and hisses loudly. Fortunately, the king cobra is extremely shy around humans.

Super stats

Scientific name: Ophiophagus hannah
Lifespan: 20 years
Length: About 13 ft (4 m)
Weight: up to 20 lb (9.1 kg)
Diet: Other snakes
Habitat: Tropical woodlands
Location: South and Southeast Asia

Weird but true!
King cobras are carnivores and like to eat other snakes, even other king cobras!

Hood for looking menacing

Smooth scales

Smooth, slender body often used for swimming

Leatherback turtle

The leatherback turtle is the largest sea turtle. Most other sea turtles have hard shells, but the leatherback has a softer, more flexible shell, a bit like leather. Its flippers are also different from other sea turtles—as it does not have claws.

Weird but true!
Leatherback turtles will travel huge distances to find their favorite food—jellyfish!

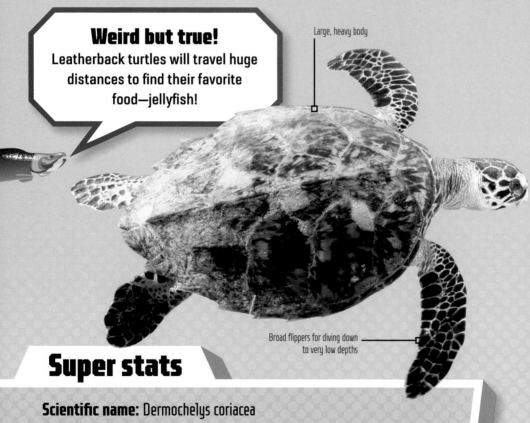

Large, heavy body

Broad flippers for diving down to very low depths

Super stats

Scientific name: Dermochelys coriacea
Lifespan: About 50 years
Length: 3–6½ ft (1–2 m)   **Weight:** 550–1,500 lb (250–700 kg)
Diet: Jellyfish and sea squirts
Habitat: Open seas
Location: All oceans except the coldest areas of the Arctic and Antarctic

Flying dragon

This tiny reptile spends most of its life in trees. It has developed a clever way of "flying" from tree to tree in search of food or a mate, or to escape a predator. It glides through the air using special flaps of skin stretched over its elongated ribs.

Super stats

Scientific name: Draco volans
Life span: 8 years
Length: Up to 8½ in (21 cm)
Weight: About ¾ oz (21 g)
Diet: Ants and termites
Habitat: Rainforest and forests
Location: Across southeast Asia, and into south India

Weird but true!

Females lay eggs on the ground, but return to the trees after about a day—leaving the young to fend for themselves!

Extendable ribs giving structure to wings

Wings for traveling up to 30 ft (9 m)

Long, slim tails for steering while flying

Five-lined skink

This reptile lives in damp, wooded areas, which provide lots of places to hide—such as cracks in rocks or leaf debris. The skink's favorite foods are found here, too, including insects, spiders, snails, and frogs.

Orange coloring found on males' snouts during the mating season

Detachable tail to distract predators

Bright blue tail of young skink

Five stripes that fade with age

Weird but true!
The skink's eggs need to be kept warm and damp, so females sometimes pee on them!

Super stats

Scientific name: Eumeces fasciatus
Life span: About 6 years
Length: 5-8½ in (12.5-21.5 cm) **Weight:** Unknown
Diet: Insects and spiders
Habitat: Moist wooded areas and forest clearings with places for cover
Location: Eastern North America

Golden tree snake

The golden tree snake can usually be found resting in tropical trees. It is also known as the golden flying snake because, when threatened, it can spread its ribs and then launch its body toward the next tree—although this is gliding, not flying.

Super stats

Scientific name:
Chrysopelea ornata
Life span: 4-12 years
Length: 3¼-4¼ ft (1-1.3 m)
Weight: Up to 2 lb (1 kg)
Diet: Frogs, geckos, bats, and small birds
Habitat: Forests, park, and gardens
Location: South and southeast Asia

Fangs to deliver venom into prey

Large eyes

Ribs that can be stretched into a curved shape for gliding

Greenish-yellow color, with black scales.

Weird but true!
The golden tree snake grips prey tightly until the venom takes effect.

Big-headed turtl

As you might guess from its name, this turtle has a big head. In fact, its head is so large that it cannot pull it back into its shell, like most other turtles. Instead, its head is covered with a separate bony protective shield.

Hard protective covering on head, called a scute

Flat, triangular head

Pointed beak containing powerful jaws

American alligator

This alligator lurks, partially underwater, in lakes, rivers, and swamps, ready to pounce on prey. Unlike other alligators, it eats more than just fish. Turtles, mammals, and even birds on low branches can all be prey.

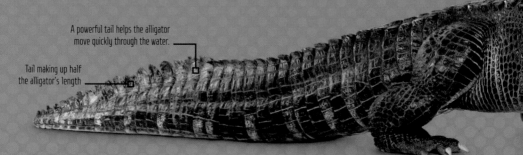

A powerful tail helps the alligator move quickly through the water.

Tail making up half the alligator's length

Super stats

Scientific name: Platysternon megacephalum
Life span: Up to 15 years
Length: Up to 15¾ in (40 cm)
Tail length: Around 7 in (17 cm)
Weight: Unknown
Diet: Fish, mollusks, and worms
Habitat: Mountain streams within forested areas
Location: Parts of Asia, including China

Scaly tail, nearly as long as turtle's body

Weird but true!

Most turtles swim a lot, but the big-headed turtle prefers climbing on land, with its strong legs and claws.

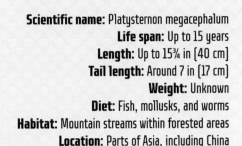

Clawed feet

Weird but true!

Unlike most reptiles, female American alligators look after their young.

Super stats

Scientific name: Alligator mississippiensis
Life span: About 50 years
Length: 9¾–16 ft (3–5 m)
Weight: 1,000 lb (454 kg)
Diet: Fish, turtles, snakes, and small mammals
Habitat: Freshwater rivers, lakes, swamps, and marshes
Location: Southeast USA

Broad snout

Webbed feet for swimming

Sea turtle

Many sea turtles only leave the ocean to lay their eggs. Although they need air to breathe, they can dive underwater for about 40 minutes at a time to search for food. However, if they are resting or sleeping, they can hold their breath underwater for up to seven hours.

Sea turtles often swim thousands of miles from their feeding areas to their special breeding area.

Sea turtles can be up to 7 ft [2.1 m] long.

Flippers help the sea turtles dive underwater to find food.

Sea turtle: Long-distance swimmer

Head-to-head!

Some animals that swim in the sea need to hold their breath underwater. Other animals can take in oxygen from the water itself! The creatures on these pages are experts at going without oxygen, but which can last the longest?

Tardigrade

These tiny animals need to "breathe" in oxygen through water to survive. But when there's no water around, they have a clever trick to keep themselves alive. Their body shuts down into a dried-out deathlike state, until they can access oxygen again.

Skin absorbs oxygen from water

Mouth for piercing plants and algae and sucking out their contents

Tardigrades are found everywhere on Earth.

Tardigrade: Indestructible wonder

Who would win?

The sea turtle can hold its breath longer than any other reptile, and better than any mammal! But it is still no match for the tiny tardigrade. This unusual creature can last for more than five years without oxygen in a dried-out state.

Winner!

253

Paradise tree snake

This tree–dwelling snake is also known as the Paradise flying snake. In fact, it can glide the farthest out of all five species of "flying" snake. It travels up to 32 ft (25 m) from one tree to another, in search of food.

Black and green body with orange, diamond-shaped markings

Bearded dragon

This lizard doesn't have an actual beard—just spiny scales under its chin. The scales puff up when the lizard feels threatened, to frighten off predators. It also puffs up its "beard" to impress mates.

Tail almost the same length as body

Strong legs

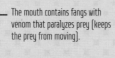

The mouth contains fangs with venom that paralyzes prey (keeps the prey from moving).

Super stats

Scientific name: Chrysopelea paradisi
Life span: Up to 10 years
Length: Up to 3 ft (0.9 m)
Weight: Unknown
Diet: Lizards, frogs, bats, and birds
Habitat: Tropical forests
Location: India, Southeast Asia, western Indonesia, and the Philippines

Weird but true!

The paradise tree snake can double its width to help it glide better.

Its ribs can be elongated (stretched out) to flatten the body for gliding.

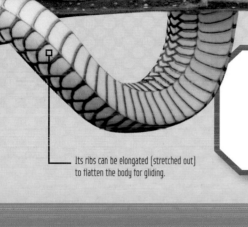

Scales can change color, often to help the bearded dragon attract a mate.

Weird but true!

Bearded dragons wave at one another to communicate.

Super stats

Scientific name: Pogona vitticeps
Life span: 10–15 years
Length: 16–20 in (40–50 cm)
Tail length: 16–20 in (40–50 cm)
Weight: 17½–18 oz (380–510 g) **Diet:** Small vertebrates, invertebrates, and plant material, including fruit and leaves
Habitat: Desert and dry woodland **Location:** Australia

Thorny devil

The spikes on this lizard are designed to protect it against predators. However, the thorny devil also uses its spikes to find water in the desert. It rubs them against plants, so that dew runs down the spikes into its mouth.

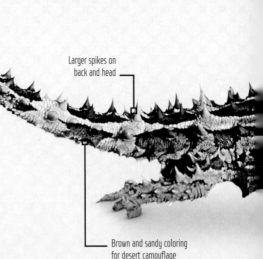

Larger spikes on back and head

Brown and sandy coloring for desert camouflage

Rough green snake

This snake lives mostly in trees near water, and it is an excellent swimmer. It gets its name from the unusual texture of its scales. Each scale has a ridge along the middle which creates a rough texture.

Excellent eyesight

Weird but true!
Rough green snakes can coil themselves up like a spring then straighten out quickly to launch themselves at prey.

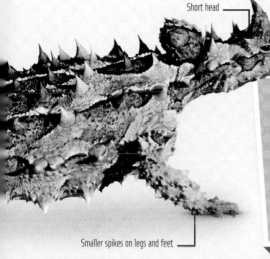

Weird but true!
A thorny devil can eat
2,500 insects in one meal!

Short head

Smaller spikes on legs and feet

Super stats

Scientific name: Moloch horridus
Life span: Up to 20 years
Length: 6-7 in (15-18 cm)
Weight: ¾-1¾ oz (25-50 g)
Diet: Ants and other insects
Habitat: Desert
Location: South and West Australia

Super stats

Scientific name: Opheodrys aestivus
Life span: Up to 8 years
Length: 2½-3¼ ft (75-100 cm)
Weight: ¼-1 ⅞ oz (9-54 g)
Diet: Invertebrates, including caterpillars, grasshoppers, and beetles
Habitat: Forests, parks, and gardens
Location: Eastern north America and Mexico

Slender body with white or yellow-green belly

Green color for camouflage amongst vegetation

California legless lizard

This creature might look like a snake, but it is actually a lizard! The two features that prove this fact are its eyelids, which snakes do not have, and that it can shed part of its tail to confuse predators—a clever lizard trick.

Slender body

Blunt tail

Namaqua chameleon

Most chameleons live in trees, but the Namaqua chameleon is specially adapted to live on the ground in the Namib desert in Africa. Its classic chameleon color-changing ability is not just for camouflage—changing color also helps it keep cool in the Sun and warm at night.

Eyes that can swivel to the back

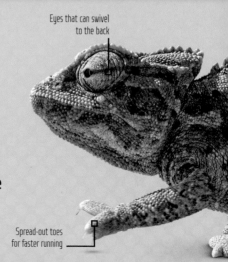

Spread-out toes for faster running

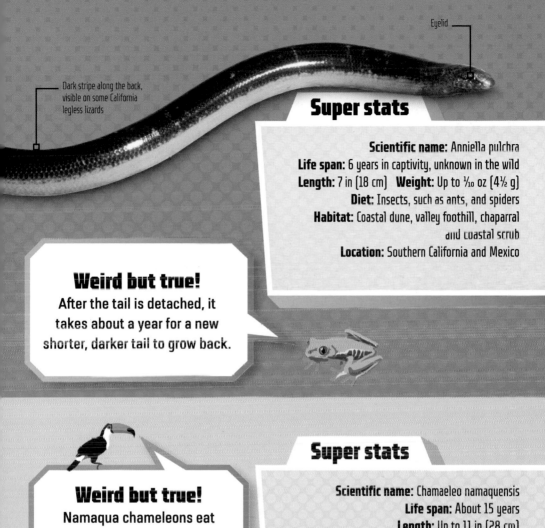

Eyelid

Dark stripe along the back, visible on some California legless lizards

Super stats

Scientific name: Anniella pulchra
Life span: 6 years in captivity, unknown in the wild
Length: 7 in (18 cm)   **Weight:** Up to 1/10 oz (4½ g)
Diet: Insects, such as ants, and spiders
Habitat: Coastal dune, valley foothill, chaparral and coastal scrub
Location: Southern California and Mexico

Weird but true!

After the tail is detached, it takes about a year for a new shorter, darker tail to grow back.

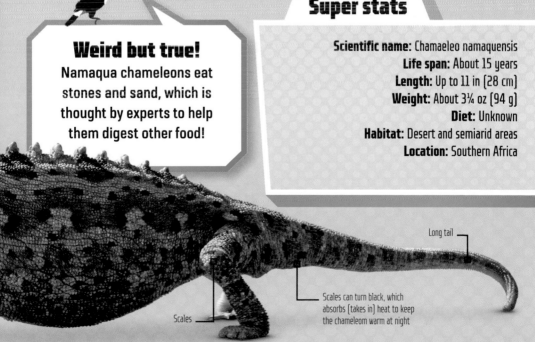

Weird but true!

Namaqua chameleons eat stones and sand, which is thought by experts to help them digest other food!

Super stats

Scientific name: Chamaeleo namaquensis
Life span: About 15 years
Length: Up to 11 in (28 cm)
Weight: About 3¼ oz (94 g)
Diet: Unknown
Habitat: Desert and semiarid areas
Location: Southern Africa

Long tail

Scales

Scales can turn black, which absorbs (takes in) heat to keep the chameleom warm at night

259

Gaboon Viper

This patient predator likes to lurk completely still on the forest floor, ready to ambush its prey. When it spots a rodent, mammal, bird, or frog it strikes quickly with its 2-in (5-cm)-long fangs.

Weird but true!
Most snakes lay eggs, but the gaboon viper gives birth to live young.

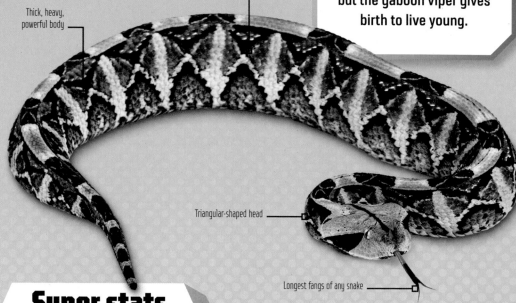

Colorful markings to blend in with forest floor

Thick, heavy, powerful body

Triangular-shaped head

Longest fangs of any snake

Super stats

Scientific name: Bitis gabonica
Life span: About 20 years
Length: About 6 ft (1.8 m) **Weight:** About 45 lb (20 kg)
Diet: Small and medium-sized mammals and birds
Habitat: Rainforest and tropical forests
Location: Central, east and west Africa

Shovel-snouted lizard

This tiny lizard is one of the few creatures that can survive the heat of the Namib desert. Its shovel-shaped snout helps it burrow deeply into the sand dunes either to "swim" away from predators or to rest in the cooler sand beneath the surface.

Body the size of a human's little finger.

Long hind legs for fast running

Short front legs used for steering.

Long tail

Weird but true!

To stop the sand from burning its feet, the shovel-snouted lizard holds one limb up at a time, like it is dancing.

Super stats

Scientific name: Meroles anchietae
Life span: Unknown
Length: About 2 in (5 cm) **Weight:** Unknown
Diet: Insects, especially small beetles
Habitat: Desert
Location: Angola and Namibia

Sandfish skink

A fish-shaped body gives this creature its name. The sandfish skink uses its streamlined body to "swim" through sand to catch its prey, to escape from predators, and to keep cool in its desert habitat.

Limbs only used overground, not for "swimming"

Tuatara

Most of the tuatara's relatives became extinct more than 100 million years ago. This rare, lizardlike species is the sole survivor of a prehistoric group of reptiles, and it can only be found on two groups of islands near New Zealand.

Long tail

Loose, scaly skin

Short, strong legs, ideal for digging burrows

Weird but true!

The sandfish skink finds prey by sensing the vibrations they cause in sand.

Super stats

Scientific name: Scincus scincus
Life span: Up to 10 years in captivity
Length: Up to 3½ in (9 cm)
Weight: Up to ½ oz (16 g)
Diet: Insects
Habitat: Deserts and dunes
Location: Egypt and North Africa

Wide, powerful body for wriggling through sand

Triangular head

Smaller lower jaw and overhanging upper jaw to avoid scooping up sand

Ears and nose partially covered by scales, to keep out sand

Super stats

Scientific name: Sphenodon punctatus
Life span: Up to 90 years
Length: About 2 ft (61 cm)
Weight: About 3¼ lb (1.5 kg)
Diet: Beetles, weta, worms, millipedes, and spiders
Habitat: Burrows
Location: New Zealand

"Third eye" on top of head, blind but sensitive to light

Spiny crest running from head to tail

Large head

Weird but true!

Tuataras live for a very long time, with some reaching more than 100 years old.

Texas thread snake

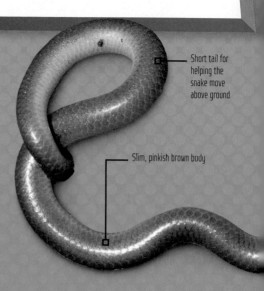

The Texas thread snake is also known as the Texas blind snake, because its tiny eyes give it extremely limited vision. This snake can only sense light, not movement. However, as it spends most of its time underground, good vision is not important.

Short tail for helping the snake move above ground

Slim, pinkish brown body

Jackson's chameleon

The three horns on this Jackson's chameleon's head show that it is male. Females have tiny horns, or none at all. The males use their horns to show off to other males and to defend their territory.

Body can be inflated to scare off predators

Long tail for wrapping around tree branches

Super stats

Scientific name: Rena dulcis
Life span: Unknown
Length: 6-10½ in (15-27 cm)
Weight: Around ⅟₁₆ oz (1.4 g)
Diet: Small insects, spiders, and larvae of ants and termites
Habitat: Burrows
Location: South USA and northeast Mexico

Tiny eyes and small head

Smooth scales

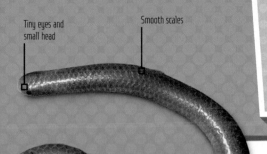

Weird but true!
Female Texas thread snakes lay up to seven eggs a time and protect them by coiling their bodies around them until they hatch.

Weird but true!
Female Jackson's chameleons can have up to 100 babies per year.

Super stats

Scientific name: Trioceros jacksonii
Life span: 2-3 years
Length: 8-12 in (20-30 cm)
Weight: 3¼-5¼ oz (90-150 g)
Diet: Insects
Habitat: Forests
Location: Kenya and Tanzania

Nose horn

Two horns above the eyes

Galápagos tortoise

Meet the largest tortoise in the world. It's also the heaviest, weighing up to 882 lbs (400kg)—as heavy as a horse! It lives on the volcanic Galápagos Islands in the Pacific Ocean, where it spends its days grazing on vegetation and basking in pools. Some can live for more than 100 years.

Classifying creatures

All the creatures of the animal kingdom are separated into groups based on their physical similarities and differences. This is called classification.

Vertebrates and invertebrates

Animals fall into one of two groups—those with a backbone, called vertebrates, and those without a backbone, called invertebrates. Bigger animals tend to be vertebrates, and smaller animals are usually invertebrates.

Vertebrates

Vertebrates can be divided up, or classified, into smaller groups, made up of animals who share certain features.

Mammals

Warm-blooded mammals are covered in hair or fur. The females give birth to live young and feed their babies milk.

Birds

These warm-blooded animals have feathers and all have beaks.

Fish

Cold-blooded fish have gills and fins which allow them to breathe and swim in water.

Amphibians

These cold-blooded animals are born in the water, but grow up to live on both land and water.

Reptiles

These cold-blooded animals have scaly skin and lay eggs.

Invertebrates

As with vertebrates, invertebrates are divided up, or classified, into smaller groups. The animals in each group share features such as hard, protective body armor.

Annelids

These are segmented worms, such as the earthworm.

Arthropods

A segmented body, exoskeleton, and paired body parts, such legs, set arthopods apart.

Cnidarians

Soft-bodied cnidarians live in marine habitats, such as the oceans.

Echinoderms

These are star-shaped marine creatures.

Mollusks

Soft-bodied mollusks are often protected by hard shells.

Poriferans

Soft-bodied poriferans are marine creatures fixed in one place.

Weird but true!

Some invertebrates join together in large numbers to form colonies.

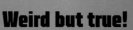

Saltwater crocodile

Saltwater crocodiles lurk at the water's edge waiting for prey such as water buffalo, monkeys, wild boar, and even sharks to take a drink. Then, they grab their prey in their jaws and drag it back into the water.

Saltwater crocodiles are excellent swimmers and can travel over 620 miles (1,000 km) by sea.

66 teeth

Up to 23 ft (7 m) long body

Saltwater crocodile: Patient predator

Head-to-head!

Mighty predators need powerful mouths to catch, kill, and eat prey. Saltwater crocodiles and great white sharks have among the most impressive jaws in the animal kingdom, but which one has the strongest bite?

Great white shark

Prey such as sea lions, seals, and small whales don't stand a chance against this fast and fierce fish. When the great white gets close to its prey, it lurches forward and chomps down with its 300 sharp teeth.

Up to 26 ft (8 m) long body

Triangular, serrated (jagged) teeth

These sharks can sniff out a colony of seals from 2 miles (3.2 km) away.

Great white shark: Super-fast sea predator

Who would win?

Along with its relative the Nile crocodile, the saltwater crocodile's bite is more than 20 times stronger than an adult human's. Compared to its size, it is also almost three times stronger than the great white, so this predator wins!

Winner!

Frilled lizard

When under attack, the frilled lizard doesn't try to escape right away. It makes itself look scary first— by opening out its neck frill, bobbing its head, lashing its tail, waving its legs, opening its mouth wide, and hissing.

Weird but true!

After finishing its fearsome display, the frilled lizard quickly climbs a tree to escape!

Super stats

Scientific name:
Chlamydosaurus kingii
Life span: Up to 20 years
Length: About 35 in (90 cm)
Weight: About 1⅛ lb (0.5 kg)
Diet: Insects and other lizards
Habitat: Subtropical woodlands
Location: Australia

Paper-thin skin forms the frill.

Open frill makes the lizard look much bigger

Long tail

Sharp claws

Black mamba

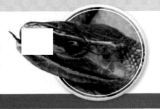

The black mamba is one of the fastest and most venomous snakes in the world. It's speedy, too—a streamlined body allows it to slither smoothly through open woodland. It can even climb trees if it needs to!

Super stats

Scientific name: Dendroaspis polylepis
Life span: At least 11 years
Length: About 14 ft (4.2 m)
Weight: About 3½ lb (1.5 kg)
Diet: Small mammals and birds
Habitat: Savannas and rocky hills
Location: South and East Africa

Weird but true!

Black mambas get their names from the black color of the insides of their mouths.

Bodies are grey or brown

Large, smooth scales

A folded-back hood can be spread out to scare off attackers.

Komodo dragon

The Komodo dragon is the largest lizard and one of the mightiest predators in the world. It uses its long, forked tongue to smell food up to 6 miles (10 km) away and swallows small prey whole. However, it can also take down animals much bigger than itself with its powerful tail before tearing them apart with its saw-edged teeth.

Long, muscular tail, used for balance and as a powerful weapon to attack larger animals

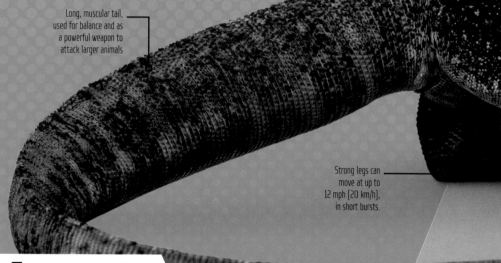

Strong legs can move at up to 12 mph (20 km/h), in short bursts.

Super stats

Scientific name: Varanus komodoensis **Life span:** Up to 30 years
Length: Up to 10 ft (3 m)   **Weight:** More than 150 lb (70 kg)
Diet: Mainly carrion, but also live deer, wild pigs, birds, goats, reptiles
Habitat: Hot, dry grasslands and tropical forests
Location: Islands of southern Indonesia

Weird but true!

A Komodo dragon can eat up to 80 percent of its own body weight in a single meal—enough to last the lizard for the whole month!

Poor night vision means the Komodo dragon relies on its sense of smell to find prey.

Heavy, bulky body

Tough, scaly skin forms a protective armor against predators, and other Komodo dragons.

Five sharp claws on each foot to help grip large prey

Forked tongue, used to taste the air in search of food

The Komodo dragon uses its 60 curved, jagged teeth to wound animals and inject them with venom, found in the lizard's saliva.

Green anaconda

Weighing about as much as a pig, this is the world's heaviest snake. It is also very long—about the same length as a school bus. The green anaconda's size means it moves slowly on land, but it is a strong swimmer. It stays hidden in water while waiting for its prey.

Females are larger than males.

Weird but true!

Stretchy jaws allow green anacondas to swallow huge prey, as big as caimans or pigs, in one gulp! They can go for months without food after a big meal.

Small head compared to the rest of the body

Eyes and nostrils high on the head, for seeing and breathing while submerged in water

Super stats

Scientific name: Eunectes murinus
Life span: About 10 years
Length: About 30 ft (9 m)   **Weight:** Up to 55 lb (25 kg)
Diet: Almost anything, including fish, reptiles, birds, and mammals
Habitat: Swamps and flooded forests
Location: Northern regions of South America

Thick waist, up to 12 in (30 cm) wide

Powerful body used to coil around prey and squeeze it to death

Olive-green skin with oval markings help the anaconda blend in with its surroundings.

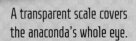

A transparent scale covers the anaconda's whole eye.

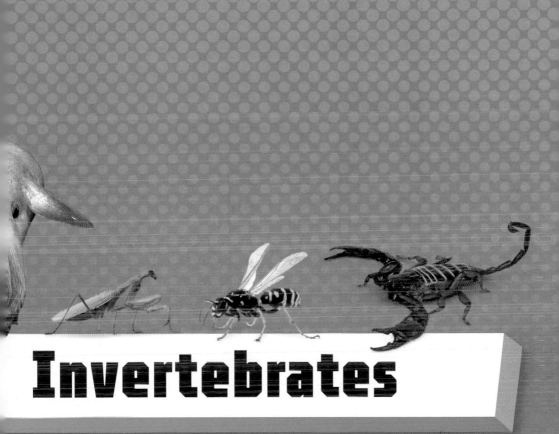

Invertebrates

Invertebrates have been around for more than 600 million years and they form the largest group of animals on Earth. In fact, about 97 percent of all the animals in the world are invertebrates, and just one family, beetles (coleoptera) make up about one quarter of all living species on the planet. Many invertebrates live in the oceans, but even more live on land. The only thing that all invertebrates have in common is that they don't have a backbone, or any skeleton inside them at all.

What is an invertebrate?

Invertebrates are animals with no backbone, and no skeleton inside them at all. About 97 percent of all the animals in the world are invertebrates. They come in many different shapes and sizes, and are found in all habitats.

What sorts of animals are invertebrates?

All sorts! Invertebrates are a huge group of animals, ranging from tiny insects to giant squid. They can be broken down into smaller family groups though, such as mollusks, insects, and worms.

The smallest invertebrates are tiny single-celled protozoans that can only be seen using a microscope.

What do invertebrates have instead of a backbone?

Some invertebrates, such as worms, have soft, flexible bodies with no bones at all. Others, such as snails are protected by hard outer shells. But most invertebrates, including insects, spiders, and crustaceans, have skeletons on the outside. They are called arthropods.

What kind of babies do invertebrates have?

Most invertebrates hatch from eggs. Some hatch as larvae—tiny creatures that look very different from the adults of their species. Others hatch as smaller versions of adults, and grow bigger over time.

Are invertebrates really found everywhere?

Yes, even Antarctica! The Antarctic midge—a tiny, flightless insect—spends most of the year frozen solid. Many invertebrates live in the oceans, though, where, the water supports their bodies and food often simply swims toward them.

281

Cobalt blue tarantula

The cobalt blue tarantula lives in deep burrows in tropical rain forests. Scientists are not sure why it is such a bright blue. Like most spiders, its eyesight is poor, so it is unlikely that the color is used to attract a mate. Instead, it may be used to warn off predators.

Weird but true!
Female cobalt blue tarantulas can live twice as long as males.

Eight eyes

This spider can appear almost black from a distance, but close up they are a distinctive bright blue.

Legs have an iridescent sheen

The fangs deliver a venomous bite that is deadly to small insects but only irritates human skin.

Super stats

Scientific name: Cyriopagopus lividus **Life span:** Up to 24 years
Weight: Unknown **Length:** About 5 in (13 cm)
Diet: Insects, other spiders, amphibians, and mice
Habitat: Tropical rain forests **Location:** Southeast Asia

European stag beetle

Stag beetles get their name from their large "horns," which look like the antlers of male deer (stags). However, they are actually huge jaws. Males use them to fight each other over territory and to impress females. Female beetles have much smaller jaws.

Super stats

Scientific name: Lucanus cervus
Life span: 3-7 years
Weight: $\frac{1}{10}$–$\frac{1}{5}$ oz (2-6 g)
Length: 3 in (7.5 cm)
Diet: Tree sap
Habitat: Forests and parks
Location: Asia and Europe

Black head and thorax

Enormous jaws

Male stag beetles are about the size of an adult human's thumb.

Dark brown wing case

The long wings are hidden under cases. Both males and females can fly, but females spend more time on the ground.

Weird but true!

Stag beetles spend up to six years as larvae that live under, and feed on, rotting wood and decaying plants.

Frog beetle

Super stats

Scientific name: Sagra buqueti
Life span: Unknown
Weight: Unknown
Length: About 2 in (5 cm)
Diet: Leaves
Habitat: Forests
Location: Southeast Asia

The long, powerful hind legs of this beetle look a bit like a frog's, hence its name. However, unlike a frog, they are not used for jumping. Instead, the frog beetle uses them, along with its gripping feet, to help climb steep surfaces.

Long antennae

Jaws are found underneath the head

Froglike legs

Weird but true!

Males have much longer and thicker legs than females. It is thought that they use their legs in wrestling contests to attract a mate.

The frog beetle has wings under its wing cases, but doesn't use them.

Thousands of tiny hairs on its feet allow the frog beetle to cling onto most surfaces.

Two-spot assassin bug

Assassin bugs are deadly hunters. They use their mouth to stab their prey and then release a toxin that paralyzes it almost immediately. The bug then sucks out its dinner's bodily fluids with its strawlike mouthparts.

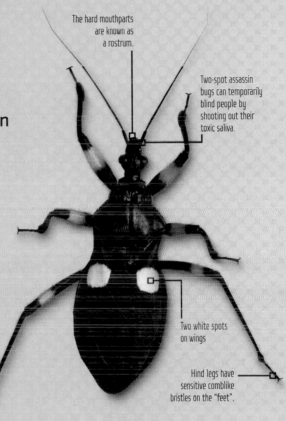

The hard mouthparts are known as a rostrum.

Two-spot assassin bugs can temporarily blind people by shooting out their toxic saliva.

Two white spots on wings

Hind legs have sensitive comblike bristles on the "feet".

Weird but true!

There are 7,000 types of assassin bug. One group, known as "bee assassins" coat their legs with sticky plant resin to catch bees.

Super stats

Scientific name: Platymeris biguttata
Life span: Up to 2 years in captivity
Weight: Unknown **Length:** 1⅝ in (4 cm)
Diet: Other insects
Habitat: Unknown **Location:** West Africa

Common Wasp

Super stats

Scientific name: Vespula vulgaris
Lifespan: Unknown
Weight: Unknown
Length: About ¾ in (2 cm)
Diet: Flies, aphids, caterpillars and other invertebrates
Habitat: Forests, meadows, and gardens
Location: UK

There are more than 30,000 species of wasps. Most, including common wasps and hornets, are black and yellow, but others can have green, blue, or red markings. Bright colors warn predators that these insects can sting!

Weird but true!
Some wasps build large, papery nests made out of chewed-up wood.

Two pairs of clear wings

Only female wasps can sting. The sting is contained in their egg-laying part (ovipositor).

Wasps have a distinctive narrow "waist" called a petiole between their thorax and abdomen.

Large eyes

Mouthparts used to bite and cut

Seven-spot ladybug

Ladybugs are brightly colored beetles. Most have spots on their wings, but there are actually about 5,000 different species of ladybugs and they come in a range of different patterns. The seven-spot ladybug is the most common type in Europe.

Pair of long wings used for flying

Oval body

Weird but true!
When attacked, the ladybug releases bitter-tasting blood from its knees.

Hard, shiny wing cases are called the elytra.

Chewing mouthparts can gobble up to 50 aphids every day.

The ladybug's bright color warns predators not to eat it.

Super stats

Scientific name: Coccinella septempunctata   **Life span:** Unknown
Weight: Unknown   **Length:** About ⅜ in (9 mm)
Diet: Other insects, particularly aphids
Habitat: Forests, parks, and gardens
Location: Asia, Europe, and North America

Common octopus

Weird but true!

When threatened, a common octopus squirts a cloud of black ink to distract and confuse its attacker and then swims away.

This clever cephalopod has many unusual talents. It is an expert in camouflage—it can change its skin color and texture to hide from predators. It has venomous saliva, a sharp bite, and can even lose an arm to escape a predator and then regrow it.

Large eyes

Mantle has a bumpy or "warty" texture.

Large, soft body (mantle) can squeeze into small cracks to hide from predators.

Body is up to 3.2 ft (1 m) long.

Each arm has two rows of suckers.

Sharp, beak-like mouth.

Super stats

Scientific name: Octopus vulgaris **Life span:** 1-2 years
Length: 12-36 in (30-91 cm) **Weight:** 6⅗-22 lb (3-10 kg)
Diet: Crabs, crayfish, and mollusks
Habitat: Tropical and temperate waters
Location: Worldwide

Giant Pacific Octopus

Meet the largest octopus, and one of the biggest invertebrate predators in the ocean. The giant Pacific octopus is a fast, agile, and intelligent hunter, preying on fish, crabs, and even sharks. It grabs its prey with its eight limbs and then immobilizes them with its venom.

Super stats

Scientific name: Enteroctopus dofleini
Life span: 3–5 years
Length: Up to 16 ft (5 m)
Weight: Up to 110 lb (50 kg)
Diet: Mostly shellfish, crabs and lobsters
Habitat: Coral reefs
Location: Pacific Ocean, from Japan to Alaska, USA

Despite its size, its soft body can squeeze through small gaps or hide in tiny crevices.

Weird but true!

Female octopuses lay around 100,000 eggs. They guard the eggs until they hatch (it takes about six months), and then die.

Each arm has two rows of large suckers to grab prey.

A giant Pacific octopus can have up to 500 suckers.

Like most octopuses, it can change its skin color to hide from predators.

Dung beetle

Meet the world's strongest insect! Some dung beetles can support more than 1,141 times their own body weight—that's like an adult human supporting six double-decker buses. And these incredible insects are useful, too. They clean up animal poo (dung) by rolling it into balls and taking it to their underground homes for their young to feed on.

Hercules beetl

Male hercules beetles have two large horns which make them more than twice the size of females. In fact, the males hercules beetle is one of the biggest beetles around. Measuring up to 6 in (15 cm) long, it is bigger than some mice!

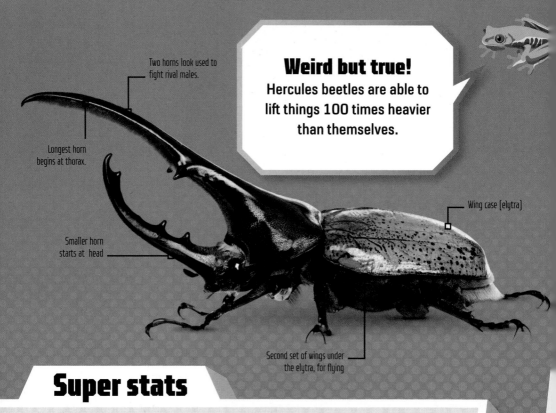

Two horns look used to fight rival males.

Longest horn begins at thorax.

Smaller horn starts at head

Wing case (elytra)

Second set of wings under the elytra, for flying

Weird but true!
Hercules beetles are able to lift things 100 times heavier than themselves.

Super stats

Scientific name: Dynastes hercules
Lifespan: 3 years
Length: Up to 6 in (17 cm)   **Weight:** Unknown
Diet: Larva eat rotting wood and adults eat fallen fruit
Habitat: Montane and tropical rainforests
Location: Central and South America

Pine weevil

Weevils are one of the largest families in the animal kingdom. They are also known as snout beetles because of their extra-long, snout-like rostrums which extend from their heads. They use these snouts to feed or to burrow inside plants and lay eggs.

Super stats

Scientific name: Hylobius abietis
Lifespan: 2-3 months
Length: ⅖-½ in (10-13 mm)
Weight: Unknown
Diet: Plant material, such as bark
Habitat: Woodland
Location: Europe

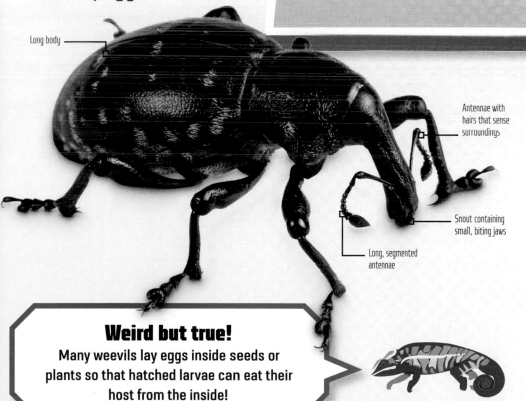

Long body

Antennae with hairs that sense surroundings

Snout containing small, biting jaws

Long, segmented antennae

Weird but true!
Many weevils lay eggs inside seeds or plants so that hatched larvae can eat their host from the inside!

Green-legged metallic beetle

It is thought that this beetle's shimmering coloring acts as a form of camouflage. The green-legged metallic beetle is a type of jewel beetle, which are named so because of their iridescent, jewellike bodies, which come in shades of green, red, purple, or blue.

Serrated (jagged) antennae

Giant clam

The giant clam is the world's heaviest shelled animal. The largest ever weighed 660 lb (300 kg), that's heavier than a pig! It doesn't move around much, and feeds by filtering plankton out of the sea. It also gets nutrients from algae that lives inside its body (mantle).

Bivalve shell – meaning it has two parts joined by a hinge

Brightly coloured wing cases (elytra)

Narrow, flat body

Abdomen tapers almost to a point.

Weird but true!
In the past, people wore jewel beetles as brooches.

Super stats

Scientific name: Sternocera aequisignata
Lifespan: About 2 years including all larvae stages — adult stage is up to 3 weeks
Length: 1–2 in (2.5-5 cm)
Weight: About 3/50 oz (1.8 g)
Diet: Plant juices and sap
Habitat: Forests, farmlands, and gardens
Location: Asia – India, Myanmar, and Thailand

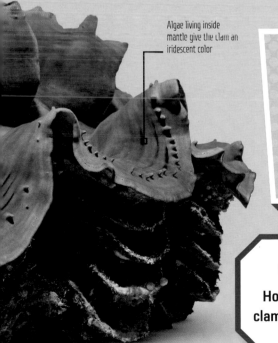

Algae living inside mantle give the clam an iridescent color

Super stats

Scientific name: Tridacna gigas
Lifespan: Up to 100 years
Length: Shell up to 4½ ft (1.4 m) across
Weight: Up to 551 lb (250 kg)
Diet: Algae and plankton
Habitat: Shallow ocean waters
Location: South Pacific and Indian Oceans

Weird but true!
Horizontal ridges on a giant clam's shell show how old it is.

atlas moth

The Atlas moth is so large that it is sometimes mistaken for a bird. With a wingspan of 10 in (25 cm), it's bigger than any other butterfly or moth— about as big as a dinner plate.

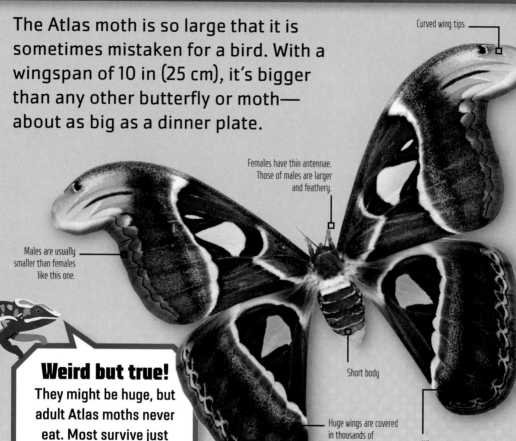

Curved wing tips

Females have thin antennae. Those of males are larger and feathery.

Males are usually smaller than females like this one.

Short body

Huge wings are covered in thousands of overlapping scales

Wing patterns are created by different colored scales

Weird but true!
They might be huge, but adult Atlas moths never eat. Most survive just long enough to breed.

Super stats

Scientific name: Attacus atlas
Life span: About 2 weeks once emerged as a butterfly
Weight: Unknown **Length:** About 11 in (27 cm)
Diet: Nothing as an adult but leaves of cinnamon, citrus fruit, guava and Jamaican cherry trees as a caterpillar.
Habitat: Rain forests **Location:** China, India, Malaysia and Indonesia

:: rlequin be tl

This large, tropical beetle has distinctive black, red and yellow markings on its wing cases. However, the most striking thing about it is its long front legs, which are often longer than its body. Males use them to attract females.

Super stats

Scientific name:
Acrocinus longimanus
Life span: About 10 years
Weight: Unknown
Length: About 3 in [7.5 cm]
Diet: Sap
Habitat: Forests
Location: Mexico to south America

Legs used to crawl over branches

Females like this one have shorter legs than males.

The harlequin beetle's patterned body helps it hide on fungus-covered tree trunks.

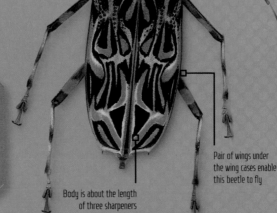

Pair of wings under the wing cases enable this beetle to fly

Body is about the length of three sharpeners

Weird but true!
Minute arachnids hitch a ride to new food sources beneath the harlequin beetle's wing cases.

Top teamwork

Leaf–cutter ants live in colonies of up to one million ants. They use their strong jaws to chop up leaves into small pieces and carry them back to their nests. They can carry leaves up to 50 times heavier than their own body weight. The leaves decay and grow fungus, and the ants eat the fungus.

Prime predators

Predators might seem like nature's villains, but they're just doing what they need to do to survive. Every creature needs to eat, and it's not easy being top of the food chain. It takes patience, skill, and cunning to be an apex (top) predator. It can be a risky business, too. Let's meet some animals that take grabbing a bite to eat to a whole new level.

Great white shark

These fearsome fish combine power and patience. They overpower their prey with a single bite from their huge jaws, and then wait for it to grow weak before starting to eat their meal.

Black widow spider

Small but dangerous, the black widow spider uses powerful venom to overpower its prey. Its venom is deadlier than many snakes.

Bald eagle

Sharp eyesight makes bald eagles top predators. From high in the sky, they scan the ground for prey and then swoop down to grab it with their sharp talons.

Lions

Teamwork is key for lions. A group of lions, known as a pride, work together to hunt and take down prey, such as zebras. Despite this, lions only succeed in about 20% of their attacks.

Polar bear

A polar bear's white fur is the perfect camouflage in its snowy habitat. They wait patiently by cracks in the ice to swipe fish or seals, and other small mammals. They may also swim long distances in search of food.

Humans

Humans are the ultimate super predators, using tools and technology to catch prey at a speed and scale that would not be possible in nature. No other animal can match that.

Komodo dragon

The world's largest lizard's body is a deadly weapon. Its combination of powerful tail, sharp claws, and venomous saliva can take down prey much larger than itself. However, Komodo dragons don't always hunt—sometimes they just feed on carrion (dead animals).

Termite

This insect is really good at teamwork. It lives in huge colonies and works together to build enormous nests. The moundlike nests are made from mud, spit, and their own droppings, and can be up to 25 ft (7 m) high. That's taller than a giraffe!

Weird but true!
Termite colonies are led by a queen, who lays up to 30,000 eggs in a single day!

Long antennae

Hornlike body parts

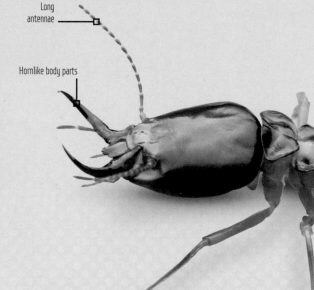

Reddish body

Super stats

Scientific name: Isoptera
Lifespan: Up to 15 years for queens
Length: Worker ⅛–¾ in (3–20 mm) and queen up to 5 in (13 cm)
Weight: Less than ⅒ lb (45 g)
Diet: Plant material, or fungus grown by termites
Habitat: Mostly on grassland   **Location:** Warm regions worldwide

Glow worm

Glow worms are actually beetles, not worms—but they do glow! Their natural light-up ability is called bioluminescence, and they use it to communicate with each other at night. Females emit a brighter glow than males and use it to attract a mate.

Weird but true!
Adults only live for a few weeks, purely to breed, and they do not eat in that time.

Nu mouthpart

Segmented body

Adult female glow worms look a lot like larvae, but they don't have the reddish spots on the edge of each segment that are visible in larvae.

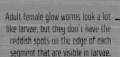

Bioluminescent glow comes from the abdomen.

Females can grow up to ¾ in (2 cm) long.

Super stats

Scientific name: Lampyris noctiluca
Life span: 2-5 days
Length: About ⅗-1 in (1.5-2.5 cm) **Weight:** About ⅛ oz (4.5 g)
Diet: Nothing as an adult, they eat slugs and snails in their larvae form
Habitat: Caves, grasslands, and woodlands
Location: Africa, Europe, Asia, and Central America

Jewel scarab

Super stats

Scientific name: Chrysina resplendens
Life span: About 3 months
Length: Up to 1 in (3 cm)
Weight: Unknown
Diet: Leaves
Habitat: High-altitude tropical forest
Location: Central America

The body of this rare scarab beetle reflects light so that it looks metallic. It lives in one of the wettest places on Earth, the mountainous cloud forests of Central America. It is also known as the golden scarab beetle or the golden chafer.

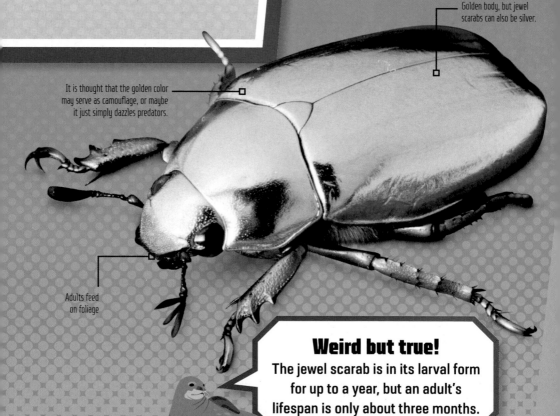

Golden body, but jewel scarabs can also be silver.

It is thought that the golden color may serve as camouflage, or maybe it just simply dazzles predators.

Adults feed on foliage

Weird but true!
The jewel scarab is in its larval form for up to a year, but an adult's lifespan is only about three months.

Black widow

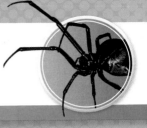

A black widow spider's venom is about 15 times stronger than rattlesnake venom, but it is not the most venomous spider in the world. (That's thought to be the funnel web spider from Australia.) However, only the females of the species are venomous.

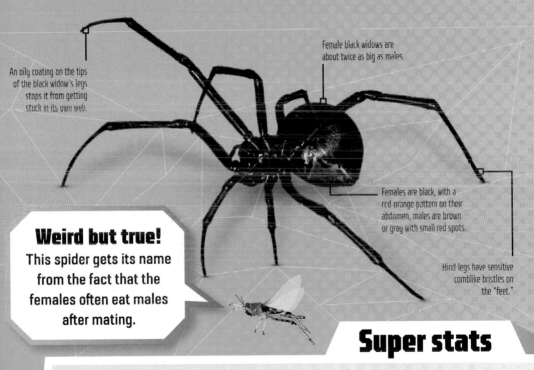

An oily coating on the tips of the black widow's legs stops it from getting stuck in its own web.

Female black widows are about twice as big as males.

Females are black, with a red orange pattern on their abdomen, males are brown or gray with small red spots.

Hind legs have sensitive comblike bristles on the "feet."

Weird but true!

This spider gets its name from the fact that the females often eat males after mating.

Super stats

Scientific name: Latrodectus
Life span: 1-3 years
Length: About 1½ in (4 cm) **Weight:** About ¹⁄₃₂ oz (1 g)
Diet: Flies, mosquitoes, grasshoppers, beetles, and caterpillars
Habitat: Temperate regions
Location: Worldwide except Antarctica

Cockroach

Cockroaches have been around for more than 320 million years. They have adapted to live anywhere warm, from tropical regions to centrally heated houses in human cities. Cockroaches are nocturnal and their favorite foods are rotting plants and animals.

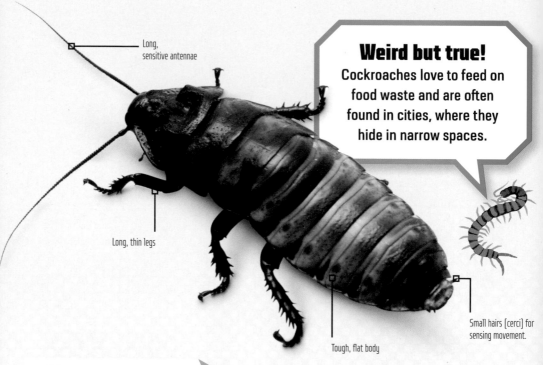

Long, sensitive antennae

Weird but true!
Cockroaches love to feed on food waste and are often found in cities, where they hide in narrow spaces.

Long, thin legs

Small hairs (cerci) for sensing movement.

Tough, flat body

Super stats

Scientific name: Blattodea
Life span: About 1.5 years as an adult
Length: Up to 2 in (50 mm)   **Weight:** Unknown
Diet: Almost anything, but especially meat
Habitat: In or near buildings containing human food
Location: Worldwide

Cicada

Cicadas are the noisiest insects in the world. They mostly live underground, and only emerge to breed. Males attract mates by vibrating drumlike pads on the sides of their abdomens. This "song" can be heard up to 1 mile (1.5 km) away.

Short antennae

Short, compact body

Brown or dark green coloring for camouflage in trees

Wings of adult cicada

Weird but true!

The African cicada (Brevisana brevis) produces a sound of 106.7 decibels, which is louder than a lawnmower.

Super stats

Scientific name: Cicadoidea
Life span: Up to 17 years
Length: ¾–2³⁄₁₀ in (1.9–5.7 cm)   **Weight:** Unknown
Diet: Sap from tree roots, twigs, and branches
Habitat: Tropical deserts, grasslands, and forests
Location: Throughout the world

Emperor scorpion

With its enormous pincers, the Emperor scorpion looks a bit like a lobster. It's actually an eight–legged arachnid, in the same family as spiders. Although it's one of the biggest scorpions, the sting in its tail is only about as powerful as a bee sting.

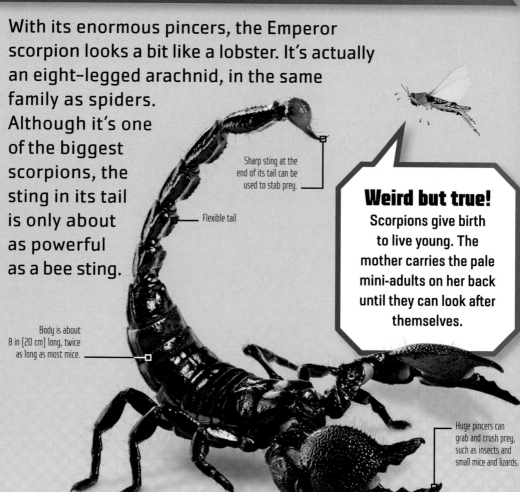

Sharp sting at the end of its tail can be used to stab prey.

Flexible tail

Body is about 8 in (20 cm) long, twice as long as most mice.

Huge pincers can grab and crush prey, such as insects and small mice and lizards.

Weird but true!
Scorpions give birth to live young. The mother carries the pale mini-adults on her back until they can look after themselves.

Super stats

Scientific name: Pandinus imperator
Life span: 5-8 years in captivity
Length: Up to 8 in (20 cm)   **Weight:** Unknown
Diet: Small animals
Habitat: Forest floor
Location: West Africa

Arabian fat-tailed scorpion

Although not the biggest scorpion, the Arabian fat-tailed scorpion is one of the deadliest. Its large, wide tail (which gives it its name) can inflict a deadly sting onto prey, such as mites, ticks, beetles, spiders, earthworms, lizards, millipedes, and even rats.

Super stats

Scientific name: Androctonus crassicauda
Life span: 3–8 years
Length: 3 ⅞ in (10 cm)
Weight: ½₂–¼ oz (0.5–5 g)
Diet: Small animals, such as insects and their larvae, and rats
Habitat: Desert and semidesert regions **Location:** North Africa and West Asia

Weird but true!
Arabian fat-tailed scorpions like to live in old or ruined buildings.

Sting is twice as powerful as many bigger scorpions.

Pincers

Adults are around 4 in (10 cm) long, about the same size as a large mouse.

Goliath beetle

The goliath beetle is the heaviest insect in the world. It is so strong that it can lift loads up to 850 times heavier than itself! It is also one of the largest insects, measuring up to 4 in (10 cm) long—that's only slightly smaller than your hand.

Super stats

Scientific name: Goliathus cacicus
Life span: Unknown
Length: 2¼–4 in (5½–10 cm)
Weight: 2¾–3½ oz (80–100 g)
Diet: Fruit, decayed leaves, bark, and sap.
Habitat: Rotting vegetation
Location: Equatorial Africa

Weird but true!
Even goliath beetle larvae are heavy. They can weigh up to 3.5 oz (100 g)—that's as heavy as two golf balls!

Y-shaped horn of the male goliath beetle, for fighting other males

These sharp claws help them climb trees.

Elytra (wing case)

D rwin's beetl

Males have huge jaws that look a bit like horns. These are longer than their bodies and used to fight other males.

Males are much larger than females.

Wing cases (elytra) are dark brown.

Body is dark green and red with an iridescent sheen and covered in short hairs.

This stag beetle is named after 19th century British biologist Charles Darwin. He collected a specimen in Argentina in around 1832, but then it got lost. Darwin's specimen was found again in 2008, but the species is so rare that biologists think that it might even be extinct.

Weird but true!
Legend has it that this beetle hit Charles Darwin. However, although it has huge jaws, its bite force is quite weak so it wouldn't have hurt too much.

Super stats

Scientific name: Chiasognathus grantii
Life span: Unknown
Length: Up to 2 ⅜-3½ in (60-90 mm)
Weight: Unknown
Diet: Dead or decayed wood for larvae and juices of trees for adults
Habitat: Temperate and subantarctic forests
Location: Argentina and Chile

Madagascan moon moth

Madagascan moon moths spend most of their lives as caterpillars, munching on plants. Adults live for only about a week and in that time their sole purpose is to mate. Females lay up to 150 eggs because many of the caterpillars will be eaten by predators, such as birds.

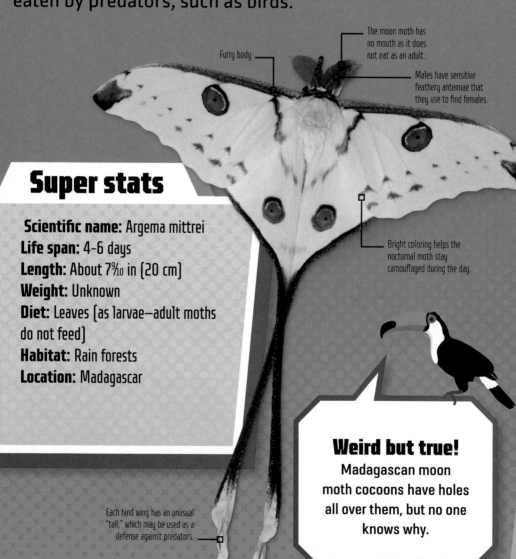

Furry body

The moon moth has no mouth as it does not eat as an adult.

Males have sensitive feathery antennae that they use to find females.

Bright coloring helps the nocturnal moth stay camouflaged during the day.

Each hind wing has an unusual "tail," which may be used as a defense against predators.

Super stats

Scientific name: Argema mittrei
Life span: 4-6 days
Length: About 7 9/10 in (20 cm)
Weight: Unknown
Diet: Leaves (as larvae—adult moths do not feed)
Habitat: Rain forests
Location: Madagascar

Weird but true!
Madagascan moon moth cocoons have holes all over them, but no one knows why.

Giraffe Weevil

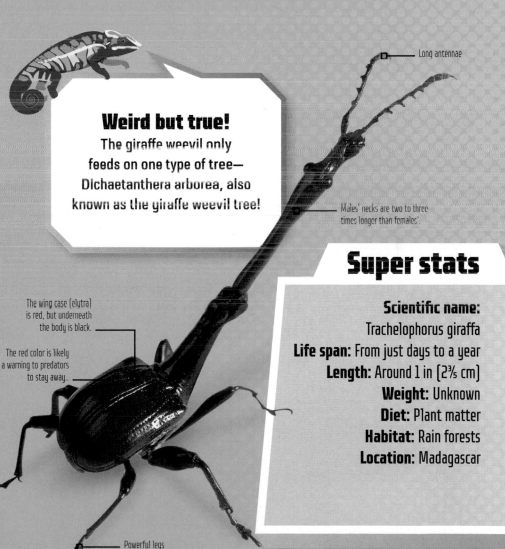

It's not hard to see why this weevil gets its name—like a giraffe, it has a very long neck. Males mostly use their necks to fight each other in order to impress a mate. Females use their necks to roll leaves around their eggs, to feed the larvae when they hatch.

Weird but true!

The giraffe weevil only feeds on one type of tree—Dichaetanthera arborea, also known as the giraffe weevil tree!

Long antennae

Males' necks are two to three times longer than females'.

The wing case (elytra) is red, but underneath the body is black.

The red color is likely a warning to predators to stay away..

Powerful legs

Super stats

Scientific name: Trachelophorus giraffa
Life span: From just days to a year
Length: Around 1 in (2⅗ cm)
Weight: Unknown
Diet: Plant matter
Habitat: Rain forests
Location: Madagascar

Humboldt squid

Meet one of the fiestiest squid in the sea. The humboldt squid lives in the waters of the Pacific Ocean. It moves in packs numbering in the thousands, hunting for fish. When angry, it turns a bright red and may even attack its companions.

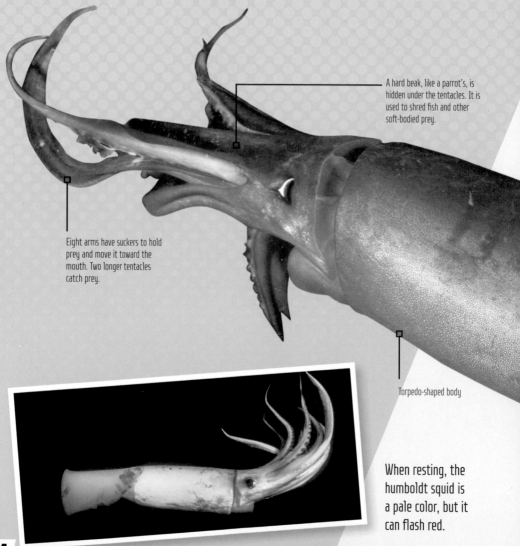

A hard beak, like a parrot's, is hidden under the tentacles. It is used to shred fish and other soft-bodied prey.

Eight arms have suckers to hold prey and move it toward the mouth. Two longer tentacles catch prey.

Torpedo-shaped body

When resting, the humboldt squid is a pale color, but it can flash red.

Super stats

Scientific name: Dosidicus gigas
Life span: About 1 year   **Weight:** 110 lb (50 kg)
Length: 6½ ft (2 m)
Diet: Other squid, crustaceans, and fish
Habitat: Ocean   **Location:** East Pacific Ocean

Weird but true!

The humboldt squid's brain is shaped a bit like a ring doughnut. It Is positioned around the tube that leads from its mouth to its digestive system.

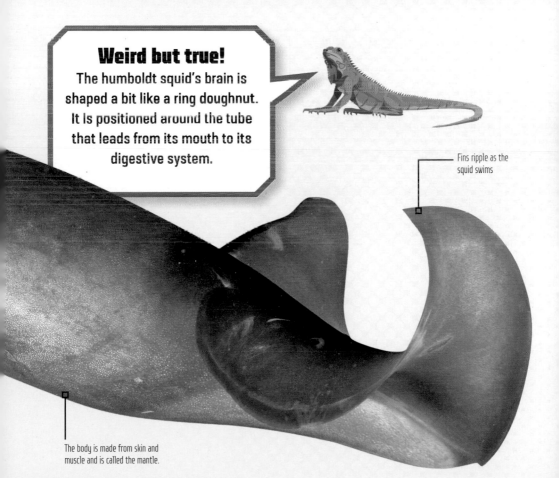

Fins ripple as the squid swims

The body is made from skin and muscle and is called the mantle.

Pacific sea nettle

This huge, golden jellyfish can swim, but it mostly moves by drifting along with ocean currents. The Pacific sea nettle uses its long, stinging tentacles to paralyze prey before reeling them into its bell-shaped body to eat them.

Weird but true!

Creatures such as fish eat the Pacific sea nettle, despite its sting!

24 long, red tentacles, each with millions of stinging cells

Jelly-like bell

Arms reel in prey

Super stats

Scientific name: Chrysaora fuscescens
Life span: Up to 1 year
Length: Up to 30 in (76 cm) across bell **Weight:** Unknown
Diet: Zooplankton and other jellyfish
Habitat: Ocean
Location: North Pacific Ocean

Greater blue-ringed octopus

This small octopus is one of the most venomous animals in the ocean. Its venom is contained in its saliva (spit). The blue-ringed octopus eithers bites prey, such as crustaceans and small fish, or simply releases its saliva into the ocean and waits.

Super stats

Scientific name: Hapalochlaena lunulate   **Life span:** Up to 2 years
Length: 4¾-8½ in (12-22 cm)
Weight: Usually up to 3½ oz (100 g)
Diet: Crabs, small fish, shrimps, and other crustaceans
Habitat: Shallow reefs, rocky areas, and coasts in tropical oceans
Location: Tropical Asia, Japan, New Guinea, and Australia

Yellow skin with around 50 blue and black rings

Body can change shape in order to camouflage itself.

Weird but true!
The octopus' rings can pulsate (expand and contract quickly) to scare off predators.

Flat rock scorpio n

This scorpion has a clever way of hiding from predators, and avoiding the heat of the desert—it squeezes its flat body between rocks. The flat rock scorpion then comes out at night, when it's cooler, to hunt for insects and other scorpions.

Long, thin tail with stinger at the end.

Flat body

Wide, flat head

It's one of the longest scorpions in the world at around 7 7/8 in (20 cm) long.

Curved claws also help this scorpion to grip onto rocks.

Eight legs are covered with small hairs to give the rock scorpion extra grip.

Long, powerful pincers can grab prey and then crush or tear it into smaller pieces.

Super stats

Scientific name:
Hadogenes troglodytes
Life span: Unknown
Length: 4-7 in (10-18 cm)
Weight: Up to 1⅛ oz (32 g)
Diet: Other scorpions, spiders, and insects
Habitat: Cracks in rocks in scrublands
Location: Botswana, Mozambique, South Africa, Zimbabwe

Weird but true!
Although its tail contains a mild venom, the rock scorpion rarely stings. Its powerful claws are a better form of attack, and defense.

Deathstalker scorpion

During the day, this nocturnal animal hides under rocks, in crevices, and even sometimes in burrows abandoned by other animals. The deathstalker scorpion is small—not even as wide as your hand—but it's venom is one of the most powerful of all scorpions.

Super stats

Scientific name:
Leiurus quinquestriatus
Life span: Up to 35 years
Length: 3⅛–4½ in (80–110 mm)
Weight: ⅟₃₂ oz (1–2.5 g)
Diet: Insects, centipedes, spiders, and other scorpions
Habitat: Stony deserts
Location: North Africa

Weird but true!

The deathstalker scorpion's venom could help humans. Chemicals in the venom are being tested to see if they can help to treat diseases, such as cancer.

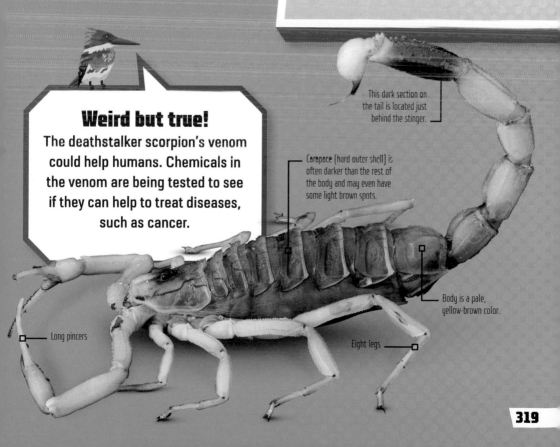

This dark section on the tail is located just behind the stinger.

Carapace (hard outer shell) is often darker than the rest of the body and may even have some light brown spots.

Body is a pale, yellow-brown color.

Long pincers

Eight legs

Barrel jellyfish

These huge jellyfish can grow to be up to 5 ft (1.5 m) long, which is about as big as a 12-year-old human. Despite their size, the barrel jellyfish's sting is not very powerful and they only eat tiny plankton and small fish.

Weird but true!
Barrel jellyfish begin life as microscopic creatures called planula.

Purple fringe containing sensory organs

Eight frilly tentacles

Super stats

Scientific name: Rhizostoma pulmo
Life span: 2–6 months
Length: Up to 4⅞ ft (1½ m)   **Weight:** Up to 77 lb (35 kg)
Diet: Plankton and small fish
Habitat: Tropical and temperate waters
Location: Worldwide

Crown jellyfish

This unusual-looking jellyfish has many names, including the crowned jellyfish and the cauliflower jellyfish. It gets its name from the unusual grooves on its body, which make it look like a crown (or cauliflower!).

Huge, translucent body

Up to 30 grooves

Up to 30 small, stinging tentacles

Weird but true!

Crown jellyfish can light up when touched, to confuse predators.

Super stats

Scientific name: Cephea cephea
Life span: Up to 6 months
Length: Unknown   **Weight:** 6⅝–22 lb (3–10 kg)
Diet: Prey on crabs, crayfish, and mollusks
Habitat: Deep tropical oceans
Location: World's oceans

Moths

Many moths have amazing hearing, but the greater wax moth beats them all. The higher the frequency of a noise, the more high pitched it sounds—and the greater wax moth can hear frequencies of up to 300 kHz! In comparison, you can only hear sounds of up to about 20kHz.

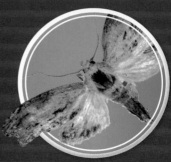

A moth may also just close its wings and drop to the floor to avoid predators.

Wax moths can be pests because they eat beeswax and other by-products of honeybees.

Moths hear using a pair of eardrumlike structures on the thorax (body).

Moth: Excellent ears

Head-to-head!

A bat makes sounds too high pitched for humans to hear. The sounds bounce off prey, such as moths, and return to the bat, telling it where the prey is. But moths can hear the bat's sounds. So which of these two species has better ears?

Bats

Bats are nocturnal animals that hunt at night, using their special sound-making and hearing abilities—called echolocation. They can not only use sound waves to find prey, but also to find out what's around them in order to navigate.

Long claws help them to hang upside down to sleep

Bats do have good eyesight, but hearing is more useful in the dark.

A bat's wing is a thin layer of skin stretched between four long fingers and a thumb.

Bat: Night-time noise detector

Who would win?

Bats have super-sharp hearing, but the winner is the greater wax moth, by some way—bats can only hear up to 200 kHz! The moth's excellent hearing helps it escape when it's being hunted at night.

Winner!

Insect camouflage

Animals have some amazing ways to protect themselves from predators, such as speed, venom, armor, color, or smell. But possibly the oldest, cleverest, and most effective way is simply to hide. Some insects have developed the most amazing camouflage. Could you spot them?

Peppered moth

This insect blends in perfectly with light-colored trees and lichens, thanks to a black and white "peppered" pattern.

Dead Leaf Butterfly

The dull underside of this butterfly's wings provides excellent camouflage. The brown color and black markings make it look just like a dead leaf.

Orchid Mantis

This insect doesn't hide from predators, it camouflages itself as a flower to fool its prey. When hungry pollinators approach, the orchid mantis strikes.

Giant swallowtail butterfly

The caterpillar larvae of the giant swallowtail butterfly has a great trick to put off predators. It camouflages itself as bird poo.

Stick and leaf insects

Camouflaging as a stick or leaf is such a good plan that at least 3,000 types of insect do it. Some really go the extra mile by swaying in the breeze or laying eggs that look like seeds.

Hoverfly

This harmless insect camouflages itself as a wasp. This puts off predators that don't want to receive a wasp sting!

Assassin bug

The assassin bug disguises itself by carrying other dead insects on its back. However, it might not be the cleverest idea as this sometimes actually attracts predators, such as spiders.

Common lobster

This armored crustacean can grow up to 3 ft (1 m) long, but it can still move pretty fast. It speeds across the ocean floor to grab prey, usually smaller invertebrates, with its huge claws.

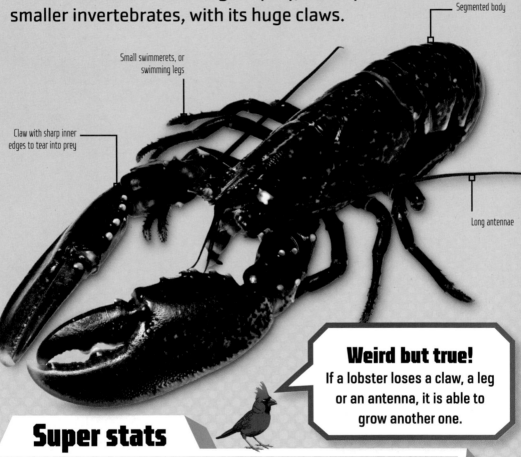

Segmented body

Small swimmerets, or swimming legs

Claw with sharp inner edges to tear into prey

Long antennae

Weird but true!
If a lobster loses a claw, a leg or an antenna, it is able to grow another one.

Super stats

Scientific name: Hamarus gammarus
Life span: More than 70 years
Length: Up to 2 ft (60 cm)   **Weight:** 20½ lb (9.3kg)
Diet: Marine invertebrates
Habitat: Crevices in rocky seabeds
Location: East Atlantic Ocean

Mimic octopus

This animal has a cunning way to avoid predators. The mimic octopus is able to change its color, shape, and behavior to mimic (pretend to be) a range of other sea creatures—from sea snakes to crabs.

Super stats

Scientific name: Thaumoctopus mimicus
Life span: Unknown
Length: Up to 2 ft [60 cm]
Weight: Unknown
Diet: Small crustaceans and fish
Habitat: Muddy river bottoms and estuary floors
Location: Indo-Pacific Ocean

Brown and white stripes

Mimic octopuses reach about 2 ft [60 cm] in length.

Weird but true!
Like other octopuses, the mimic octopus has three hearts.

Eight long, narrow limbs

Coconut octopus

Also called the veined octopus, the coconut octopus might be the cleverest member of the cephalopod family. It uses coconut shells as protective armor as it "walks" along the sandy sea floor. If there aren't any coconuts, it might use a clam shell for shelter instead.

Weird but true!
The coconut octopus is also really good at hiding. It hides its whole body under the sand on the sea floor, with only its eyes visible.

Brown body with darker brown veinlike lines

A coconut octopus can "walk" on two of its tentacles, while the rest carry the coconut shell.

Suckers along each tentacle help the octopus hold onto its prey.

Super stats

Scientific name: Amphioctopus marginatus
Life span: 3-5 years
Length: 6 in (15 cm) **Weight:** Around 14 oz (400 g)
Diet: Crabs, clams and shrimps
Habitat: Shallow seas, in sand and mud
Location: Indian and west Pacific Oceans and the Red Sea

Lion's mane jellyfish

With a body about half the size of a car, the lion's mane jellyfish is one of the largest jellyfish in the world. It can swim, but it usually just drifts with the currents, preying on any animals that get trapped in its long, stinging tentacles.

This "mane" of long, hairlike tentacles, along with its golden color gives this jellyfish its name.

Including tentacles, the biggest lion's mane jellyfish can be longer than a blue whale.

Its bell-shaped body is about 6.5 ft (2 m) wide.

These "oral arms" are special tentacles that transport prey to the mouth.

Weird but true!

The lion's mane jellyfish produces light so it can glow in the dark underwater. This is called bioluminescence.

Super stats

Scientific name: Cyanea capillata
Life span: 1 year as an adult
Length: Bell up to 7½ ft (2⅓ m) wide; Tentacles up to 121 ft (37 m) long
Weight: About 200 lbs (90 kg)   **Diet:** Fish and other jellyfish
Habitat: Cold open-ocean waters
Location: North Atlantic and North Pacific Oceans

Box jellyfish

It's not the biggest jellyfish, but the box jellyfish is one of the most dangerous creatures in the sea. Darts on its many tentacles contain fast-acting venom, which stuns or kills prey.

Its box-shaped body is light blue and transparent.

Clusters of six eyes can also be found at each corner.

Super stats

Scientific name: Chironex sp.
Life span: About 12 months
Length: Bell up to 12 in (30 cm) wide; Tentacles up to 10 ft (3 m) long
Weight: Up to 4⅜ lb (2 kg)
Diet: Fish and other planktonic animals
Habitat: Tropical and subtropical open ocean waters
Location: Worldwide

The box jellyfish uses its tentacles a bit like a fishing line to catch its prey.

15 tentacles hang from each corner of the jellyfish.

Weird but true!

The box jellyfish is also known as the sea wasp, but its sting is much more powerful and can be very dangerous to humans.

Dumbo octopus

This octopus is named after a famous movie elephant with big ears. While Dumbo the elephant used his ears to fly, the Dumbo octopus uses its ear-shaped fins to swim and to hover just above the sea floor. Webbing between its arms also helps it swim and steer.

Super stats

Scientific name: Grimpoteuthis sp.
Life span: 3-5 years
Length: Up to 6 ft (1.8 m)
Weight: Up to 13 lb (5.9 kg)
Diet: Copepods, isopods, bristle worms, and amphipods
Habitat: Deep ocean
Location: North Atlantic and North Pacific Oceans

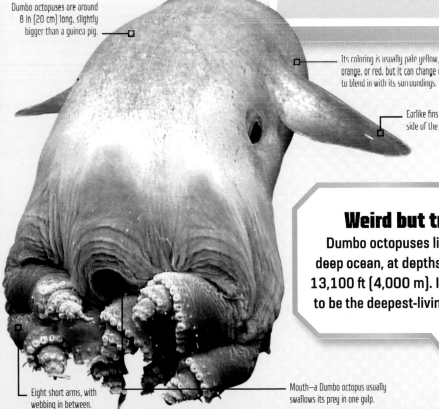

Dumbo octopuses are around 8 in (20 cm) long, slightly bigger than a guinea pig.

Its coloring is usually pale yellow, orange, or red, but it can change color to blend in with its surroundings.

Earlike fins are attached on either side of the mantle (body).

Eight short arms, with webbing in between.

Mouth—a Dumbo octopus usually swallows its prey in one gulp.

Weird but true!
Dumbo octopuses live in the deep ocean, at depths of around 13,100 ft (4,000 m). It is thought to be the deepest-living octopus.

Metamorphosis

Mammals, reptiles and birds are born looking like small versions of adults and then grow and develop as they get older. However, many invertebrates and some amphibians look quite different when they are born and go through a process called metamorphosis in which their bodies change very dramatically.

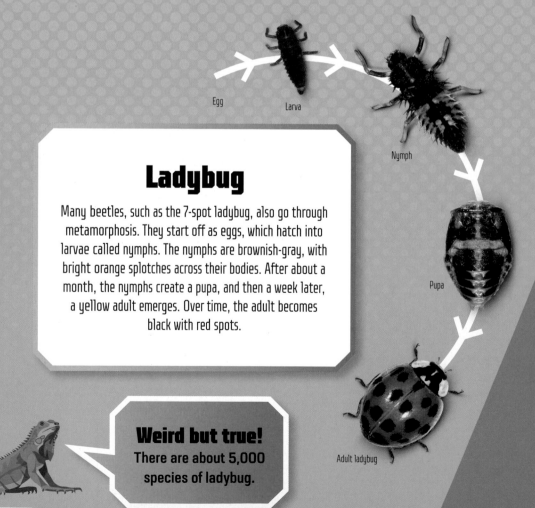

Egg

Larva

Nymph

Pupa

Adult ladybug

Ladybug

Many beetles, such as the 7-spot ladybug, also go through metamorphosis. They start off as eggs, which hatch into larvae called nymphs. The nymphs are brownish-gray, with bright orange splotches across their bodies. After about a month, the nymphs create a pupa, and then a week later, a yellow adult emerges. Over time, the adult becomes black with red spots.

Weird but true!
There are about 5,000 species of ladybug.

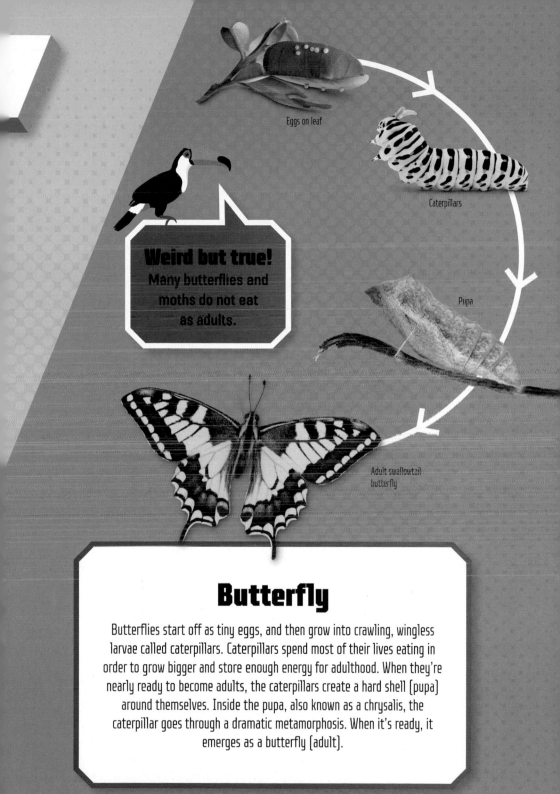

Eggs on leaf

Caterpillars

Pupa

Adult swallowtail butterfly

Weird but true!
Many butterflies and moths do not eat as adults.

Butterfly

Butterflies start off as tiny eggs, and then grow into crawling, wingless larvae called caterpillars. Caterpillars spend most of their lives eating in order to grow bigger and store enough energy for adulthood. When they're nearly ready to become adults, the caterpillars create a hard shell (pupa) around themselves. Inside the pupa, also known as a chrysalis, the caterpillar goes through a dramatic metamorphosis. When it's ready, it emerges as a butterfly (adult).

Violin beetle

The violin beetle is a type of ground beetle, which is the largest group of beetles. Its large, flat wing cases give it a distinctive silhouette, like a violin. A flattened body allows this beetle to live in small cracks and crevices.

Long antennae used to feel for prey

Elongated head

Weird but true!
Violin beetles use their long head to search under peeling bark for insect larvae to eat. Yum!

Wing cases are partly see-through, with a ridged pattern.

Long legs

The flat wing cases hide a pair of wings, but the violin beetle prefers to walk.

Super stats

Scientific name: Mormolyce phyllodes   **Life span:** 3 years including larvae stage. Adult stage is 1 year
Length: Around 4 in (10 cm)   **Weight:** Unknown
Diet: Other insects and snails
Habitat: Rain forests   **Location:** Southeast Asia

Acorn weevil

Weevils are beetles with long snouts or unusual body shapes. The acorn weevil has a long, curved snout with tiny jaws at the end, which it uses for feeding. Females have longer snouts than males and use them to drill into acorns to lay their eggs inside.

Super stats

Scientific name: Curculio glandium
Life span: Around 2.5 years
Length: Around ³⁄₁₀ in (8 mm)
Weight: Unknown
Diet: Leaves, flowers, and nuts
Habitat: Forests
Location: North America, asia and Europe

Nut-brown body helps camouflage the beetle.

Strong legs have clawed feet and are useful for scurrying through vegetation.

This male weevil's snout is long, but a female's is even longer.

Antennae have rounded club at the ends.

Jaws used to chomp on buds and leaves

Weird but true!
Acorn weevil larvae hatch inside the nut and then eat it. They then burrow into the ground, where they turn into adults.

Gray's leaf insect

Leaf insects can be hard to spot because they look a lot like leaves. This helps them avoid predators, although it does sometimes cause other insects to try and nibble them! Gray's leaf insect lives in tropical regions and is usually green to match the vegetation around it.

Females have wings, but cannot fly.

Flat body is shaped like a leaf.

Females are larger than males.

European mantis

The European mantis is more commonly known as the praying mantis due to the position it holds its front legs. It is a deadly predator, using its powerful, spiky legs to grab prey before biting off their heads and eating them.

Green body blends in with surroundings

Back legs are thinner than front legs

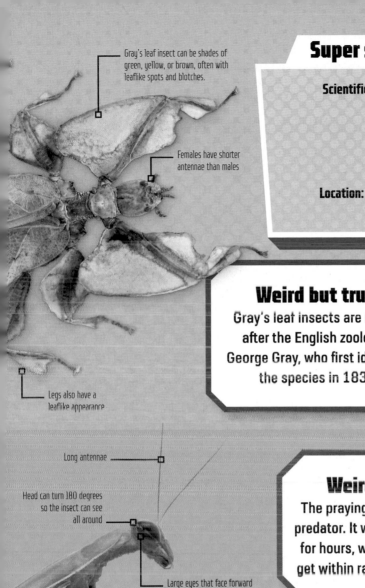

Gray's leaf insect can be shades of green, yellow, or brown, often with leaflike spots and blotches.

Females have shorter antennae than males

Legs also have a leaflike appearance

Super stats

Scientific name: Pulchriphyllium bioculatum
Lifespan: Up to 7 months
Length: About 4 in (10 cm)
Weight: Unknown
Diet: Leaves
Habitat: Rain forests
Location: Asia and islands in the Indian Ocean

Weird but true!

Gray's leaf insects are named after the English zoologist, George Gray, who first identified the species in 1832.

Long antennae

Head can turn 180 degrees so the insect can see all around

Large eyes that face forward allow the insect to tell how far away prey is.

Weird but true!

The praying mantis is a patient predator. It will sit absolutely still for hours, waiting for its prey to get within range. Then it strikes!

Spines on the front legs help the mantis to hold prey.

Super stats

Scientific name: Mantis religiosa
Life span: About 1 year in captivity, unknown in the wild
Length: About 3 in (7½ cm) **Weight:** About ¼ oz (5 g)
Diet: Other insects
Habitat: Forests **Location:** Europe and USA

337

Animal extinction

Since humans appeared on Earth, many species of animals have become extinct—which means they no longer exist. Modern animals that are risk of becoming extinct are called endangered. Here are a few of the things humans do that put animals under threat.

Hunting

Some animals are valued for their meat or body parts, such as horns and tusks. Poachers hunt and kill them in order to get hold of these things. Some animals have been hunted to extinction, or to near extinction.

Rhinoceroses are hunted for their valuable horns. All five rhino species are now endangered, some of them critically.

Pollution

Human activity can introduce dangerous chemicals into nature, called pollutants. Burning fuels pollutes the air, burying trash introduces chemicals into soil, and water can be polluted by sewage. All of these things have a negative impact on plants and animals.

Farmers use pesticides to kill insects that eat their crops. However, the pesticides also kill off honeybees, which don't eat crops.

Red panda numbers are falling because the forests they live in are being chopped down.

Beluga sturgeon are caught for their eggs, called roe. People have caught so many of them that the species is now critically endangered.

Deforestation

Trees and forests are cut down to make space for buildings and farmland and so that the trees can be used for wood. This deforestation leads to habitat loss—the animals that once lived in the forests have nowhere to go.

Overfishing

Fish are a useful source of food, and humans have caught them for thousands of years. However, some fish species are now under threat because we have caught so many of them. This means there are fewer left to produce young.

American gray squirrels were introduced to Ireland and Great Britain in the 1870s. They have almost replaced native red squirrels.

Climate change

We burn fuel to make electricity, power our vehicles, and to keep us warm. This releases gases into the air that trap heat and makes the planet warm up. Problems caused by global warming include oceans rising to flood land, after ice caps melt into the water.

Invasive species

As people travel around the world, we take animals with us, either by accident, for example if they sneak onto ships, or on purpose. Some of these "invasive" species affect animals already living in their new habitats, for example by eating their food.

The waters off North America are now too warm for lobsters to live in, which has forced them to move farther north.

Save the animals!

Animals all over the world are struggling due to humans and our actions. But all is not lost! Here are some of the ways people are trying to save the animals, and a few things you can do to help them yourself.

Vehicle engines release carbon dioxide into the air.

Watch your footprint!

Your daily activities might be causing the release of global-warming causing gases, such as carbon dioxide. The amount of carbon dioxide you produce is called your carbon footprint. One of the ways you can reduce it is by walking or cycling instead of driving or using renewable energy to heat your home.

Ocean-living animals can get tangled up in plastic bags and other plastic waste.

Use less plastic

Plastic takes thousands of years to rot away. So, plastic trash is all over our planet, including in the oceans. Animals can die if they eat it, or if they get tangled up in it. Using as little plastic as possible can help stop this problem from getting worse.

The Arabian oryx became extinct in the wild in 1972. It was bred in captivity and reintroduced into the wild in 2009.

Farm animals use space that was once available to wild animals.

Captive breeding

Sometimes, it can be too late to save a species from extinction in the wild. But animals from that species can still exist in zoos or wildlife parks, bred by humans. These may be released into the wild.

Eat less meat

The forest homes of many wild animals can be destroyed to make way for animal farms. Farm animals also burp out gases that cause global warming. Eating less meat can help solve these problems.

Orangutans are endangered because the rain forest they live in is being cut down to make space for palm oil plantations.

Beavers became extinct in the UK in the 16th century. In 2009 they were reintroduced into the Knapdale forest in Scotland.

Save the rain forest!

Many of the things we use such as some chocolates and soaps include an ingredient called palm oil. Huge areas of rain forest are cleared to make way for palm oil palms. To help stop this, you can try to buy products made with sustainable palm oil, or none at all.

Rewilding

Human activities, such as cutting down trees to clear land for buildings, have often affected wildlife—sometimes causing animals to no longer exist in an area. Some people think that rewilding will help the plants and animals in a habitat to thrive and grow. This means leaving plants to grow and bringing back animals to an area where they once lived.

Glossary

abdomen
Belly of an animal

amphibians
Vertebrates with cold blood and moist skin that can live in water or on land, and that lay their eggs in water, such as frogs, newts, salamanders, and toads

ancestor
Type of animal from the past that is related to an existing animal

antennae
Sense organs, used by insects to find food and feel their surroundings, also known as feelers

arachnids
Animals that have eight legs and two body segments, such as spiders and scorpions

backbone
Linked bones forming a columnn inside some animals, which allows them to stand or sit, also called a spine

birds
Vertebrates that lay eggs and have feathers and beaks, many of which have the ability to fly, such as parrots; others, such as ostriches and penguins, cannot fly

camouflage
How animals blend into their environment so that they cannot be seen

carapace
Hard upper part of a shell, such as that of a crustacean or tortoise

carcass
Dead body of an animal

carnivore
Animal that eats other animals

carrion
The remains of dead animals after they have been partially eaten by other animals

cell
Tiny building block of an organism

chemical
Substance created when two or more particles, such as atoms, react together

classification
Way of organizing animals into groups, based on features that they share

colony
Large group of the same type of animal, such as ants, that lives together

coral reef
Colorful, underwater structure made from the skeletons of marine animals and tiny animals called corals

crustacean
Animal with jointed legs and a tough outer shell, such as lobsters, crabs, and shrimp

dorsal fin
Body part on the back of most fish, which helps keep them upright in the water

environment
The area or surroundings in which an animal lives

evolved
Changed over a long period of time

exoskeleton
Skeleton on the outside of an animal's body

extinct
When a type of animal no longer exists

fish
Vertebrates that live in water and use gills to take in oxygen from the water, such as seahorses, clownfish, and sharks

foliage
Leaves of trees or other plants

food chain
Animals in an environment organized by what other animals they eat, with those that aren't eaten by any other animals at the top

frog
Type of amphibian with smooth skin and long back legs used for jumping

gland
Organ that makes substances that are released into the body or onto the skin for different purposes, such as sweat to help an animal cool down

habitat
Type of environment that an animal or plant calls home

herbivore
Animal that eats plants

hibernation
Sleeplike state that some animals go into during the winter months, to save energy when food is scarce

horn
Hard, pointed growth found on the heads of some animals

invertebrates
Animals without a backbone, such as jellyfish, insects, and octopuses

larvae
Young of some animals that hatch from eggs and appear different from their parents until they are mature, such as caterpillars

lichens
Organisms formed from fungi and algae, which work together to stay alive

life span
Length of time for which an animal lives

lungs
Pair of organs inside some animals that allows oxygen to enter the blood, and takes an unused gas called carbon dioxide from the blood, to be breathed out through the mouth

mammals
Warm-blooded animals that have hair or fur, a backbone, and that produce milk for their young, such as apes and elephants

marine
Term used to describe animals that live underwater

mate
Another animal of the same species, or, occasionally, a similar species, with which an animal makes babies

mollusks
Invertebrates with shells, found on land and in water, such as snails

newt
Type of amphibian, with a long tail and flat body

nutrients
Chemicals that make up food and that animals use for growth and to repair their bodies

omnivore
Animal that eats fungi, plants, and other animals

organ
Body part made up of cells, which performs a certain task, such as the lungs

organism
Living thing, such as an animal or plant

oxygen
Gas found in the air and water, which animals need to survive

paralyze
To cause an animal's muscles to stop working so that they are partly or completely unable to move

plankton
Very small animals and plants that live in water, and drift rather than swimr

poisonous
When an animal can produce harmful chemicals to hurt or kill other animals

predators
Animals that hunt and eat other animals

prey
Animals that are hunted and eaten by predators

primates
Group of mammals including chimpanzees and humans

receptors
Body part that receives sense information, such as smell or taste

reptiles
Cold-blooded vertebrates that live on land and have scaly skin, such as lizards and snakes

rodents
Group of mammals including mice and rats

salamander
Type of amphibian, with a long tail, similar to a newt

shellfish
Animals with a hard outer shell and no backbone, which live underwater

silt
Fine sand or soil carried along by flowing water and deposited on the water's bed

species
Group of animals with some characteristics in common, which can often mate to produce young together

streamlined
Smooth shape that allows easy movement through water or air

subtropical
Areas located near tropical regions, which have a warm and wet climate

temperate
Type of forest found In mild climates, which is usually made up of deciduous trees that lose their leaves in autumn

thorax
Middle part of an insect's body, between the head and the abdomen

toad
Type of amphibian very similar to a frog, but with drier skin and that spends less time in water

transluscent
Partially see-through

tropic
Hot and humid region near the Equator

vegetation
Plant life found in a particular area, or plant life in general

venom
Harmful chemical produced by some animals that can be injected into other animals through a sting or fangs

venomous
When an animal can inject a harmful liquid using stingers or fangs

vertebrates
Animals that have a backbone or spine

wingspan
Length between the tips of both wings

Index

R

rain forests 31, 50, 73, 83, 196, 212, 282, 341

ravens, common 212-13

rays
  cownose 148
  giant manta 142-3
  spotted eagle 130

reindeer 61

reproduction 11

reptiles 10, 230-77

rewilding 341

rhinoceroses 338

robins 189

S

salamanders
  Chinese giant 100-1
  European fire 106-7
  mandarin 91
  mudpuppies 114-15
  olms 114-15
  red 96

saltwater 124

scales 10, 26, 111, 125, 233, 239, 254-5, 256

scent markings 11, 20, 53

scorpionfish, tassled 142-3

scorpions
  Arabian fat-tailed 309

deathstalker 319
  emperor 308
  flat rock 318

sea kraits, banded 236-7

sea lampreys 138

sea turtles 252, 253
  green 231, 240
  leatherback 246

seahorses 124
  long-snouted 146

seals, harbor 38-9

secretary birds 183, 189

seeds 188

senses 10

sharks 124, 125, 128
  Australian ghost 152-3
  great white 166-7, 270, 271, 300
  Greenland 164, 165
  zebra 152-3

shoebills 207

shrews
  American pygmy 76, 77
  Etruscan 62-3

skeletons
  amphibians 84
  birds 173
  fish 125, 160, 222
  invertebrates 279, 280, 281
  mammals 13, 14

skin

amphibians 83, 84
  mammals 13, 14
  reptiles 233

skinks
  five-lined 248
  sandfish 262-3

sliders, yellow-bellied 234

sloths, brown-throated 31

slow worms 242-3

smell, sense of 30, 102

snailfish, Mariana 157

snails 10, 281

snakes 236-7, 245, 260, 273, 276-7
  golden tree 249
  paradise tree 254-5
  rough green 256-7
  Texas thread 264-5

sounds 64, 307, 322

sparrows 188

speed 24-5, 190, 200-1, 218

spiders 281, 282
  bird-dropping 110
  black widow 300, 305
  Sydney funnel-web 140, 141

springboks, Cape 24-5, 46

squid
  giant 280
  Humboldt 314-15

squirrels, gray 339

starlings 189, 225

Acknowledgments

DK would like to thank the following people for their assistance in the preparation of this book:

Mohd Zishan, Simran Lakhiani, Ann Cannings, Charlotte Milner and Bettina Myklebust Stovne for additional design support; Manisha Njithia and Olivia Stanford for additional editorial support; Sophia Danielsson-Waters for proofreading; and Sumedha Chopra for additional picture research.

The publisher would like to thank the following for their kind permission to reproduce their photographs:

(Key: a-above; b-below/bottom; c-center; f-far; l-left; r-right; t-top)

1 Depositphotos Inc: lilothlita [crb]. Dreamstime.com: Faunus3sd [cra]; Isselee [cra]. 2 Alamy Stock Photo: Dirk Funhoff / imageBROKER [c, t]. Dreamstime.com: Gan Chaonan [cla]. 3 Alamy Stock Photo: Steve Bray. 4 Dreamstime.com: Vasyl Helevachuk [br]. Isselee [cra]. Getty Images / iStock: GlobalP [tr]. 5 Alamy Stock Photo: Jack Goldfarb / Design Pics Inc [clb]; Bill Gozansky [br]. Dreamstime.com: Sakda Nokkaew [cra]; Harvey Stowe [cra/Swordfish]. Getty Images: wildestanimal / Moment Open [br]. Shutterstock.com: Holger Kirk [cla/Frog]; kholid mustar [bl]. 6 Dreamstime.com: Amwu [cra]; Zenobillis [cla]; Buttonhill [cra/Lizard]. naturepl.com: Afla (r/a/Owl). 7 123RF.com: Eric Isselee / isselee [cra]. Alamy Stock Photo: blickwinkel / B. Trapp [tl]. Dreamstime.com: Vojce [cla]. 10 Dreamstime.com: Isselee [cra]; Verastuchelova [cla]; Vladvitek [crb]; John Kasawa [tl]. 11 Alamy Stock Photo: Joe Blossom [clb]. Depositphotos Inc: bunwat3000 [tr]. Dreamstime.com: Isselee [tl]; Passakorn Umpornmaha [cra]. 12 Alamy Stock Photo: Rudmer Zwerver [tr]. Dreamstime.com: Anankkml [c]; Vasyl Helevachuk [c]. 13 Dreamstime.com: Anankkml [c]; Alexey Kuznetsov [r/t]; Gerra [cr]; Isselee [tcr]. 14 Dorling Kindersley: Colin Keates / Natural History Museum, London [cla]. Dreamstime.com: Isselee [bl]. 15 Dreamstime.com: Liumangtiger [cra]; Goce Risteski [cla]. Getty Images / iStock: annebaek [cb]. 16 Alamy Stock Photo: Leonello Calvetti [cra, tr]. 34 Depositphotos Inc: slowmotiongli [c, t]. 35 Dreamstime.com: Anankkml [c, b]. 36-37 Dreamstime.com: Vasyl Helevachuk [t]; Planetfelicity [cb]. 38 Alamy Stock Photo: Glenn Bartley / All Canada Photos [c]. Dreamstime.com: Vladimir Melnik / Zanskar [cb]. 40 Depositphotos Inc: izanbar [c, t]. 41 Alamy Stock Photo: Arto Hakola [c]. 42 Dreamstime.com: Isselee [tr, b]. 44-45 Dreamstime.com: Dragoneye [c]; Isselee [tr]. 46-47 Getty Images: George Pachantouris / Moment. 48 Alamy Stock Photo: Imagebroker [c, t]. 49 Alamy Stock Photo: Minden Pictures [bc]. Getty Images: Pat Gaines [br]. 50 Dreamstime.com: Marco Tomasini [c]. 51 Dreamstime.com: Isselee [tr, r]. 52-53 123RF.com: nrey. 52 123RF.com: nrey [tl]. Dreamstime.com: Musat Christian [bc]. 54 Getty Images / iStock: owngarden [b, t]. 55 Getty Images: Lea Scaddan / Moment [tr, t]. 56 Dreamstime.com: Friedemeier [tl]. 57 Shutterstock.com: Inger Eriksen [b, tr]. 59 123RF.com: Jakov Filimonov / jackf [tr, c]. Dreamstime.com: Michal Sarauer [tl, c]. 61 Dreamstime.com: Marcin Wojciechowski [tr, c]. 62-63 Alamy Stock Photo: Rudmer Zwerver [b]. naturepl.com: Dietmar Nill [t]. 64 Dreamstime.com: Slowmotiongli [cb]. Getty Images / iStock: Jeff McCurry [cra]. 65 Alamy Stock Photo: drferry [cr]. 66 Alamy Stock Photo: Tierfotoagentur [b, t]. 67 Dreamstime.com: Anankkml [b, tr]. 68-69 Alamy Stock Photo: WaterFrame [b]. 68 Alamy Stock Photo: Nature Picture Library [bl]; WaterFrame [t]. 70 123RF.com: Eric Isselee / isselee [tl]. Alamy Stock Photo: Alexey Kuznetsov [cra]; Sergey Taran [cla]. 71 Dreamstime.com: Callipso88 [cra]; Pragasis Wannapiroj [tl]; Vladvitek [clb]; Yurasova [br]. 72 Alamy Stock Photo: Steve Bray [cr, tr]. 74 Dreamstime.com: Isselee [tl]. 75 Dreamstime.com: Hongqi Zhang (aka Michael Zhang) [t, tr]. 76 Science Photo Library: E.R.Degginger [c, tr]. 77 Dreamstime.com: Melinda Fawver [c, tl]. Science Photo Library: E.R.Degginger [b]. 78 Dreamstime.com: Anankkml [c, t]. 79 Dreamstime.com: Josip Matanovic [tr, b]. 80 Dreamstime.com: Adancegiedi [tl, c]. 81 Dreamstime.com: Anankkml [b, tr]. 82 Alamy Stock Photo: Dirk Funhoff / imageBROKER [cra/Snake]; Stephen Dalton [c]. 83 Alamy Stock Photo: Bill Gozansky [c]. Dreamstime.com: Isselee [c]. 84 Dreamstime.com: Michiel De Wit [c/b]. Shutterstock.com: Federico Crovetto [crb]. 85 Dreamstime.com: Isselee [c]; Brian Magnier [cl, cla, cra, tr]. Getty Images / iStock: Izold [clb]; Scacciamosche [crb]. 86-87 Alamy Stock Photo: Dirk Funhoff / imageBROKER [c]. 87 Dreamstime.com: Lukas Blazek [cr]. 88-89 Dreamstime.com: Witr [c]. 88 Dreamstime.com: Witr [cr]. Getty Images / iStock: trino72 [tl]. 90 Dreamstime.com: Isselee [c, tl]. 91 Shutterstock.com: Fidali [cb, tr]. 92 Getty Images / iStock: Philippe Jouk [cra]. 92-93 Getty Images / iStock: Philippe Jouk [c]. 93 naturepl.com: Thomas Marent [br]. 94 Shutterstock.com: kholid mustar [c, tr]. 95 Alamy Stock Photo: Oliver Thompson-Holmes [c]. Depositphotos Inc: hendyjmp99@gmail.com [tl]. 96 Alamy Stock Photo: Bill Gozansky [c, tl]. 97 Dreamstime.com: Sergey Kolesnikov [c, tr]. 98 Alamy Stock Photo: Jack Goldfarb / Design Pics Inc [c, tl]. 99 Dreamstime.com: Holger Kirk [c, tr]. 100-101 Biosphoto: Daniel Heuclin [c]. 100 Biosphoto: Daniel Heuclin [tl]. 102 123RF.com: Martin Voeller [cl]. 123RF Premium [c, tl]. 103 123RF.com: 123RF Premium [br]. Dreamstime.com: Isselee [c, tl, br]. 104-105 Dreamstime.com: Freebilly. 106-107 Dreamstime.com: Dirk Ercken [b]; Kamensky [tr]. 106 Dreamstime.com: Dirk Ercken [cr]; Kamensky [tl]. 108 Dreamstime.com: Hotshotsworldwide [cr, tl]. 109 Dreamstime.com: Mrbenard [tr, c]. Dreamstime.com: Isselee [crb]; Marion Wear [clb]. Shutterstock.com: Jansen Chua [t]. 111 Alamy Stock Photo: BoxerX [clb]. Shutterstock.com: Berth Swanson [clb]. Dreamstime.com: Isselee [cla]. Getty Images: Animal Search [tr]. 112 Getty Images / iStock: Philippe Jouk [c]. 113 Dreamstime.com: Sharoff Owl [cr]. Shutterstock.com: Lan [c, tr]. 113 Dreamstime.com: Sharoff Owl [tr]. Duncan Noakes [c, t]. 114-115 Alamy Stock Photo: E.R. Degginger [cra]; Nature Picture Library [c]. 114 Alamy Stock Photo: E.R. Degginger [tl]; Nature Picture Library [cra]. 116-117 Alamy Stock Photo: Stuart Wilson / Biosphoto [t]. Dreamstime.com: Farinoza [b]. 116 Alamy Stock Photo: Stuart Wilson / Biosphoto [tl]. Dreamstime.com: Farinoza [clb]. 118 Getty Images: Paul Starosta / Stone [c, t]. 119 Science Photo Library: K Jayaram [tr, b]. 120-121 naturepl.com: Stephen Dalton [c]. 120 naturepl.com: Stephen Dalton [tl]. 122 Dreamstime.com: Vassiau Kolevski [t]; Sakda Nokkaew [c]; Dima Smaglov [cr]. 123 Dreamstime.com: Arsty [c]. Getty Images / iStock: irin717 [cr]; spursai [cla]. 124 Dreamstime.com: Siarhei Nosyrea [c]. 125 Alamy Stock Photo: chimages [c]. Dreamstime.com: Aleksey Alekhin [cra]; Johannesk [clb]; Steven Melanson [cla]. 126-127 Getty Images: Brandi Mueller / Moment Open. 128 Getty Images / iStock: irin717 [tl, c]. 129 Alamy Stock Photo: Helmut Corneli [tr, c]. 130 Dreamstime.com: Perfentievamarga [tl, c]. 131 Shutterstock.com: Daniel Huebner [b, tr]. 132 Dreamstime.com: Isselee [tr, clb]. 133 Getty Images / iStock: spursai [tr, b]. 134-135 Dreamstime.com: Serg dibrova [b].

134 Dreamstime.com: Frantic00 [tr]; Serg dibrova [clb]. 137 Depositphotos Inc: lilothlita [tr, c]. 138 Dreamstime.com: Arsty [c, t]. 140 Alamy Stock Photo: Imagebroker [c, tl]. 141 Getty Images / iStock: Yann-Hubert [c, tr]. Shutterstock.com: Yann hubert [br]. 142-143 Dreamstime.com: Richard Carey [t]; Dima Smaglov [bc]. 142 Dreamstime.com: Richard Carey [tl]; Dima Smaglov [clb]. 144 Alamy Stock Photo: David & Micha Sheldon / Fbonline digitale Bildagentur GmbH [c, tr]. 145 123RF.com: Oleksandr Lytvynenko [c/b, t]. 146 Dreamstime.com: Voislav Kolevski [tl, c]. 147 Dreamstime.com: Mikhail [c, tr]. 148 Dreamstime.com: Jelena Maximova [cra, tl]. 150 Dreamstime.com: Sakda Nokkaew [tl, c]. 151 Getty Images: burnsboxco [tr, c]. 152-153 Dreamstime.com: Whitcomberd [br]. naturepl.com: Doug Perrine [tc]. 152 Dreamstime.com: Whitcomberd [cr]. naturepl.com: Doug Perrine [tl]. 154-155 Dreamstime.com: Harvey Stowe [c]. 154 Dreamstime.com: Harvey Stowe [cr]. 155 Dreamstime.com: Lunamarina [br]; Izanbar [c, tr]. 157 Alamy Stock Photo: Adisha Pramod [c, tr, b]. 158 Dreamstime.com: Chernetskaya [br]. Getty Images / iStock: Imajor [tl]. 159 Dreamstime.com: Isselee [tr]; Nerfy [c]. 160-161 Alamy Stock Photo: Minden Pictures [c]. Dreamstime.com: Mirkorosenau [bc]. 160 Alamy Stock Photo: Minden Pictures [tl]. Dreamstime.com: Mirkorosenau [bc]. 162-163 Getty Images: Cynoclub [b]. 162 Dreamstime.com: Cynoclub [bc]. 164 Getty Images / iStock: Bbevren [c, t]. 165 Alamy Stock Photo: WaterFrame [c, b]. 166-167 Getty Images: by wildestanimal / Moment Open [t]. 167 Alamy Stock Photo: Brandon Cole Marine Photography [b]. 168-169 Dreamstime.com: Ozgur Guven [c]. 168 Dreamstime.com: Ozgur Guven [tl]; Michael Sluk [bc]. 170 123RF.com: Cliff Collings [c]. naturepl.com: Afla [cr]. 171 Dreamstime.com: Maria Itina [cla]; Galyna Syngaievska [cr]; Elliott Paul [cra]; Fotolia: Stefan Zeitz / Lux [cl]. 172 Dreamstime.com: Gan Chaonan [bl]; Natallia Yaumenenka [crb]. 173 Dreamstime.com: Rinus Baak [cra]; Jessamine [clb]; Mihail Ivanov [tr]; Lanasafoto [cl]. 174-175 Alamy Stock Photo: Minden Pictures [c]. 174 Alamy Stock Photo: Minden Pictures [cla]. 175 Getty Images / iStock: Mzphoto11 [br]. 176 Dreamstime.com: Lee Amery [c]; Martin Holverda [r]. 177 Shutterstock.com: Philip Pilosian [cr]. 177 Dreamstime.com: Antartis [tl]; Neal Cooper [br]; Luca Nichetti [bl]. Getty Images / iStock: Etienne Outram [c]; Rixipix [cla]. 178 Dreamstime.com: Scott Jones [tl, c]. 179 123RF.com: Cliff Collings [tr, c]. 180 Fotolia: Stefan Zeitz / Lux [tl, c]. 182 Dreamstime.com: Vladvitek [tl]. 184-185 Getty Images / iStock: Jackf. 184 Getty Images / iStock: Jackf [tl]. 185 Alamy Stock Photo: Donna Ikenberry / Art Directors [b]. 186-187 Alamy Stock Photo: Kevin Elsby. 188 Dorling Kindersley: Roger Tidman [cra]. Getty Images / iStock: Antagain [cla]. 189 Dreamstime.com: Ondavis [cla]. Getty Images / iStock: Gleb Ivanov [cr]; microgen [cla]. 190 naturepl.com: Pete Oxford [tr]. 190 Dreamstime.com: Maria Itina [tr, c]. 191 Dreamstime.com: Kabagarmah [tr, c]. 192 Dreamstime.com: Olga Lesmane [tr, c]. 193 Getty Images: Chisato Yonemochi / Afla [tr]. naturepl.com: Afla [cb]. 194 Dreamstime.com: Rigoni Barbara [t]; Sarajut Thaneerat [tr]. 195 Dreamstime.com: Sarajut Thaneerat. 196 Dreamstime.com: Zenobillis [tl, c]. 199 Dorling Kindersley: Frank Greenaway / National Birds of Prey Centre, Gloucestershire [tl, c]. 200 Dreamstime.com: Sander Meertins [c, tr]. 201 Alamy Stock Photo: Nature Picture Library [c, tr, b]. 202 Alamy Stock Photo: 3 & L Suhnis / imageBROKER [c]. 203 Alamy Stock Photo: Michael Nolan / robertharding [tr, c]. 204-205 Getty Images: Mark Chapman / 500px Plus [t]. Shutterstock.com: Francois Loubser [b]. 204 Getty Images: Mark Chapman / 500px Plus [tl]. Shutterstock.com: Flowrakisala [clb]. 206 Dreamstime.com: Flowrakisala [tl, c]. 207 Getty Images / iStock: Francois Loubser [clb/owl]. 208-209 Getty Images: Vincent Pommeyrol / Moment. 210 Dreamstime.com: Voislav Kolevski [tl]. Alamy Stock Photo: Charles Melton [tr, c]. 212-213 Getty Images / iStock: Ryzhkov Sergey [t]. 212 Getty Images / iStock: Passakorn 14 [tl]; Ryzhkov Sergey [t]. 214 Dreamstime.com: Brian Kushner [c, tr]. 215 Dreamstime.com: Brian Kushner [br]. Shutterstock.com: Gerald Robert Fischer [c, tl, bc]. 216 Dreamstime.com: Brigida Soriano [tl, c]. 217 Dreamstime.com: Chris Hill [tr, c]. 219 Shutterstock.com: Senit Fuangnakhon [bl, tr]. 220 Getty Images / iStock: Andrew Howe [tl, c]. 221 Dreamstime.com: Ecophoto [tr, b]. 223 Dorling Kindersley: Stephen Oliver [clb]. Getty Images / iStock: vukuzmin [cr]. Fotolia: Olena Pantiukh [tr]. 224 Dreamstime.com: Isselee [c, t]. 225 Dreamstime.com: Isselee [tr, c]. 226 Chris Wiley: [c, t]. 227 Alamy Stock Photo: Blickwinkel [c, t]. 228-229 Alamy Stock Photo: Chris Willson [c]. 228 Alamy Stock Photo: Chris Willson [tl]. Getty Images: Picture by Tambako the Jaguar [bc]. 230 Alamy Stock Photo: Eng Wah Teo [c]. Dreamstime.com: Amwu [cl]; Buttonhill [c]. 232 Shutterstock.com: Somedaygood [crb]. 233 Dreamstime.com: Jmrocek [cl]. 234 Dreamstime.com: Amwu [c, tl]. 235 Dreamstime.com: Buttonhill [c, t]. 236-237 Dreamstime.com: Alexey Kuznetsov [b]. 236 Dreamstime.com: Alexey Kuznetsov [clb]. 238 Alamy Stock Photo: Image Quest Marine [c]. 239 Dreamstime.com: Matthijs Kuijpers [bc, tr]. 240 Dreamstime.com: Shane Myers [c, t]. 242-243 Dreamstime.com: Amwu [bc]; ViterB [cra]. 242 Dreamstime.com: Amwu [cl]; ViterB [tl]. 245 Dreamstime.com: Isselee [b, tr]. 246 Alamy Stock Photo: Anthony Grote [c, tr]. 247 Dreamstime.com: Jiri Hrebicek [b, tr]. 248 Dreamstime.com: Senft Schubert [c, tr]. 249 Alamy Stock Photo: ephutocrop [cb, t]. 250-251 Dreamstime.com: Isselee [b]. 250 Dreamstime.com: Isselee [clb]. 252 Science Photo Library: Eye Of Science [c, tl, br]. 254-255 Alamy Stock Photo: Eng Wah Teo [c]. Dreamstime.com: Lana Langlois [bc]. 254 Alamy Stock Photo: Eng Wah Teo [tl]. Dreamstime.com: Lana Langlois [cb]. 256-257 Dorling Kindersley: Twan Leenders [bc]. Dreamstime.com: Rafael Ben Ari [cl]. 256 Dorling Kindersley: Twan Leenders [cl]. Dreamstime.com: Rafael Ben Ari [cl]. 258-259 Dreamstime.com: Ken Griffiths [bc]. naturepl.com: Visuals Unlimited [c]. 259 Dreamstime.com: Ken Griffiths [cla]. naturepl.com: Visuals Unlimited [tl]. 260 Dreamstime.com: Isselee [bc]. 261 Shutterstock.com: Chantelle Bosch [c, tr]. 264-265 Alamy Stock Photo: All Canada Photos [c]. Dreamstime.com: Amwu [b]. 264 Alamy Stock Photo: All Canada Photos [cla]. Dreamstime.com: Amwu [clb]. 266-267 Alamy Stock Photo: robertharding. 268 123RF.com: Eric Isselee / isselee [cb]. Dreamstime.com: Amwu [bc]; Kazoka [bl]; Nejron [cr]. Getty Images / iStock: Marrio31 [cr]. 269 Dorling Kindersley: Colin Keates / Natural History Museum, London [c]. 270 Dreamstime.com: Cammeraydave [clb]; Marzolusna [c]; Dirk-jan Mattaar [bl]. Getty Images / iStock: Placebo365 [clb].

270 Dreamstime.com: Volodymyr Byrdyak [c, t]. 271 Dreamstime.com: Volodymyr Byrdyak [br]; Michael Valos [c, t]. 272 Dreamstime.com: I Wayan Sumatika [b, tl]. 273 Dreamstime.com: Lucian Coman [b, tr]. 274-275 Getty Images / iStock: GlobalP [c]. 274 Getty Images / iStock: GlobalP [tl]. 275 Getty Images / iStock: AYImages [bc]. 277 Alamy Stock Photo: Juniors Bildarchiv GmbH [c]. 278 Alamy Stock Photo: NOAA [ftr]. Dorling Kindersley: Liberty's Owl, Raptor and Reptile Centre, Hampshire, UK [c]. Dreamstime.com: Faunus3sd [cla]; Apisit Wilaijit [crb]. 279 123RF.com: Eric Isselee / isselee [c]. Alamy Stock Photo: blickwinkel / B. Trapp [cr]. Dreamstime.com: Roman Samokhin [c]. 280 123RF.com: Tim Hester / timhester [ca]. Alamy Stock Photo: Maximilian Weinzierl [cr]. Dreamstime.com: ViterB [clb]. 281 Alamy Stock Photo: Blickwinkel [cra]. Dreamstime.com: John Anderson [br]; Ecophoto [tl]; Aleksandar Grozdanovski [tc]; Stephen Bonk / Sbonk [clb]. 282 Dorling Kindersley: Liberty's Owl, Raptor and Reptile Centre, Hampshire, UK [tl, c]. 283 Dreamstime.com: Thomas Eder [tr, b]. 284 Dreamstime.com: Surachai2 [tl, c]. 285 Dreamstime.com: Isselee [tr, c]. 286 Dreamstime.com: Roman Samokhin [b, tl]. 287 Getty Images / iStock: Antagain [c, tr]. 288 Alamy Stock Photo: Martin Strmiska [c, tl]. 289 naturepl.com: Brandon Cole [tr, c]. 290-291 Dreamstime.com: Neal Cooper. 292 Dreamstime.com: Isselee [c, tl]. 293 Dreamstime.com: Roman Ivaschenko [c, tr]. 294-295 Dreamstime.com: Apisit Wilaijit [ca]. Getty Images: imageBROKER / Norbert Probst [bc]. 294 Dreamstime.com: Apisit Wilaijit [tl]. Shutterstock.com: Vojce [cl]. 296 Getty Images / iStock: Chopa [c, tl]. 297 Getty Images / iStock: Hemera Technologies / PhotoObjects.net [bc, tr]. 298-299 Alamy Stock Photo: Nature Picture Library. 300 Dreamstime.com: Serju24 [crb]. 302 Dorling Kindersley: Liberty's Owl, Raptor and Reptile Centre, Hampshire, UK [tl, c]. 303 Getty Images: Julian Gunther [cr]. Shutterstock.com: Steven Giles [clb]. 301 Dreamstime.com: Sergey Uryadnikov / Surz01 [tr]; Dmytro Konstantynov [clb]. 302 Shutterstock.com: PK289 [tl, c]. 303 Alamy Stock Photo: David Chapman. Getty Images / iStock: GlobalP [tr, c]. 304 Alamy Stock Photo: Michael & Patricia Fogden / Minden Pictures [b, tl]. 305 123RF.com: peterwaters [c, t]. 306 Getty Images / iStock: strikers98 [c, tl]. 307 Getty Images / iStock: flyingv43 [tr, c]. 308 Dreamstime.com: Isselee [c, tl]. 309 Shutterstock.com: Cyrus Matiga [tc, tr]. 310 Dreamstime.com: Poerli Won [tr, tl]. 311 Alamy Stock Photo: Francisco Martinez-Clavel Martinez [c, tr]. 312 Dreamstime.com: Faunus3sd [c, tl]. 313 Dorling Kindersley: Frank Greenaway / Natural History Museum, London [bl, tr]. 314-315 Alamy Stock Photo: WaterFrame [c]. 314 Alamy Stock Photo: WaterFrame [tl, bl]. 316 Getty Images / iStock: OlGaP [cr, b]. 318 Alamy Stock Photo: Blickwinkel / B. Trapp [c, tl]. 319 Shutterstock.com: Protasov AN [b, tr]. 320 Shutterstock.com: Lidia fotografie [cr, c]. 321 Alamy Stock Photo: Reinhard Dirscherl [cl, tr]. 322 Alamy Stock Photo: Francisco Martinez-Clavel Martinez [c, tr]. 323 Alamy Stock Photo: Rudmer Zwerver [c]. 324 Alamy Stock Photo: Nature Photographers Ltd [c]; Wildlife GmbH [bl]. Dreamstime.com: Yulan [cr]. 325 Alamy Stock Photo: Biosphoto [tr]. Dreamstime.com: Isselee [cla, clb]. Shutterstock.com: Tyler Fox [cra]. 326 Dreamstime.com: Edward Westmacott [c, t]. 327 Dreamstime.com: Ethan Daniels [c, tr]. 328 Shutterstock.com: Andrey Nekrasov [cr, tr]. 330 Alamy Stock Photo: WorldFoto [cr, tl]. 331 Alamy Stock Photo: NOAA [bl]. Dreamstime.com: Palex66 [ca, clb, crb, l/crb, 2/crb]. 333 123RF.com: Miroslaw Kijewski [cr]. Dorling Kindersley: Dave King / Natural History Museum, London [tc]. Dreamstime.com: Bushalex [cra]. 334 Alamy Stock Photo: World History Archive [cr, tl]. 335 Alamy Stock Photo: Graham Prentice [cb, tl]. 336-337 123RF.com: Feathercollector [c]. 337 123RF.com: Eric Isselee / isselee [cl]. Dreamstime.com: Feathercollector [tl, b]. Bluetoes57 [bl]. 339 Alamy Stock Photo: Nreg [c]. Dorling Kindersley: Leonid Serebrennikov [tc]. Dreamstime.com: Getty Images / iStock: AB Photography [t]. 340 Dreamstime.com: Josephine Julian Lobijin [tr]; Vacamon [c]. 341 Dreamstime.com: Capa34 [tr]; Jnjhuz [crb]. Getty Images / iStock: ArefR [t]; richcarey [clb]. 342 Dreamstime.com: Dragoneye [cla]. 343 Dreamstime.com: Verastuchelova [t]. 344 Dreamstime.com: Passakorn Umpornmaha [tr]. 345 Dreamstime.com: Isselee [br]. 347 Shutterstock.com: Francois Loubser [c]. 348 Dreamstime.com: Amwu [bl]. 349 Dreamstime.com: Alexey Kuznetsov [tl]. Dreamstime.com: Dragoneye [br]. 352 Alamy Stock Photo: Nigel Dennis / Avalon.red [b].

Cover images: Front: Dreamstime.com: Amwu clb, Bennymarty tr, Isselee c, Kamensky crb, Kazoka tl, Voislav Kolevski ftl, Sombra12 cb / [flamingo], Brigida Soriano ftr, ViterB cr; Getty Images: burnsboxco cra. Back: 123RF.com: Nreg tc; Dorling Kindersley: Liberty's Owl, Raptor and Reptile Centre, Hampshire, UK cb/ [tarantula]; Dreamstime.com: Callipso88 clb/ [Horse], Gan Chaonan crb, Ozgur Guven cb, Isselee cra/ [Caracal], cla, cb, John Kasawa bc, Palex66 cla/ [Ladybug], Serg dibrova bl, Passakorn Umpornmaha tl, ViterB cl, Vladvitek cra, Poerli Won cr; Getty Images / iStock: Marrio31 tr; Spine: Dreamstime.com: Friedemeier t.

All other images © Dorling Kindersley